A Daylon C. Clark

PUBLISHING COMPANY

LORD Why Are My THIGHS Not Like HERS??

A 30 Day Journey
To Freedom From Insecurities

WENDY PAYNE

INCLUDES 125 INSPIRATIONAL CHALLENGES

A Daylon C. Clark Publishing Company
www.daylonclark.com

1   8

FIRST PRINT EDITION
Copyright © 2018 Wendy Payne
All rights reserved.

Two versions of Scripture are used in this book:
English Standard Version (ESV) © 2007 - 2018
New International Version (NIV) © 1978 - 2018

LIBRARY AND ARCHIVES CANADA DATA
ISBN: 978-0-9940643-4-9

Written and Designed in Canada. Printed in USA.

Foreword

"A flash of blonde hair and a big smile blew by me one summer day at church and right away I wanted to know the name of this very happy individual. It was Wendy Payne and the more I heard about her, the more I was intrigued to find out how she came to be the Pastor in one of our churches

There was a story there for sure because what began as a sad tale of a church closing it's doors, was now an account of a community excited to be part of this fast growing congregation. At the centre of the narrative is Pastor Wendy Payne, lover of God, daughter of the King, wife, Mom, Grandma, friend, whirlwind. Her contagious exuberance for loving Jesus has permeated her community and her church family. Wendy is passionate about life in general, and about her family and Jesus in particular. She's a beautiful woman full of energy with a desire and calling to love individuals to the Kingdom of God. She is a woman led by the Holy Spirit, a blogger, a speaker . . . someone you'll want to call friend."

–Debbie Gibbons
PAOC WOD Ministry Womens Coordinator

Endorsements

"Filled with exclamation marks and "HAHAHAs", Wendy's writing blurts out the truth of our vulnerabilities, insecurities, and fears - and then invites us to see ourselves through God's eyes. Practical reminders (wear a rubber band on your wrist for a week), written prayers and simple Scriptures will guide you through 30 days that have the potential to genuinely transform your thinking!"

–Patti Miller
Lead Pastor: Evangel Church, Montreal Quebec

"Now here is a lady that, "tells it like it is".... No flowery words just the bare facts! Wendy writes from a true deep down place many fear to tread. In doing so I believe you will be encouraged to face the deep hidden areas of your lives that you have kept hidden far too long. Ladies, get ready, as you read through this daily devotional & use the work pages to record your progress, I believe you'll one day look back and be amazed at how far you've come, possibly you'll even feel ready to help someone else on their journey!"

–Sherry Watkinson
Women's Connection Muskoka Section Team Leader

Endorsements

"Let's be honest, don't we all want those perfect thighs along with happy homes, peaceful work places, relief from stress? You may not be an early morning person or welcome the discipline of a study time but just a reading a few pages from Wendy Payne's new book will have you hooked and on your way to a revolutionized life!

Wendy cuts to the heart of our true selves, exposing our weaknesses, fears, battles and she challenges us to give God permission to work in us and transform our lives. Make no mistake, this is not your ordinary devotional book ... you'll know the author's bra size in just a few chapters! Her book is a breath of fresh air because Wendy is not afraid to be honest and transparent about her own journey. No more second guessing, she has overcome negativity and her fears and now motivates us to reach beyond our self perceived abilities and address our toughest questions.

I liked reading about Wendy's personal journey as she addresses the crucial issues with which we're confronted - I could relate! and I think you will too. She examines what women need to keep their faith strong in spite of the distractions they face and even better, she provides the tools to be successful. Each daily devotion comes with:

A Truth To Stand On
A Prayer for Today
A Daily Challenge!

Things I Learned About Myself Today
This book has the capability to change your life if you look deep within yourself while using the tools provided, and allow God to transform you daily as you follow the example of Jesus in Luke 5:16, and 'come away to pray' . . . and read!!"

–Debbie Gibbons
PAOC WOD Ministry Womens Coordinator

Acknowledgements

I am so thankful to my incredible family; my husband Darrel and my girls Natasha, Vanessa, Tamara and my son-in-law Joshua. They are the most supportive family a woman could ever have. You are my biggest cheerleaders constantly encouraging and pushing me forward. Words cannot express how truly blessed I am to have you in my life. I will never know

Edited by:
Patti McKenzie

Published by:
Daylon C. Clark

Table Of Contents

Introduction

Dear Friend,

Walk with me along this journey of overcoming our insecurities together. Often, we feel alone in our thoughts and feelings on this topic. I am here to show you that you are not alone.

In this devotional I share very raw and real situations that I experienced in my life. It has been an incredible journey of coming to the realization the purposes and plans that my Saviour Jesus Christ has for me. As I have walked this journey and allowed Him to speak into my life, He has brought healing to my mind, soul and spirit. I am overwhelmed and honoured that He would have me share this with you!

I believe this is a divine appointment for you!!! Today is your day to begin a new victorious journey in your own personal life!

As you read each day's devotional be sure to take the time to complete each daily challenge.

Allow the Lord to speak into your heart and show you just how incredible He truly thinks you are!

Thank you for giving me the opportunity to speak into your life! I pray my story encourages you, as well as speaks life into your heart. I look forward to hearing the victorious testimonies as you allow the Lord to build you up to be the strong tower He created you to be!

Wendy Payne

LORD Why Are My THIGHS Not Like HERS??

Wendy Payne

DAY 1

How Did It All Begin?

How Did It All Begin?

Truth To Stand On:

I will give thanks to you, for I am fearfully and wonderfully made: wonderful are your works, and my soul knows it full well.
–Psalms 139:14 (ESV)

Anxiety, self-doubt, hesitancy; These words are synonyms for insecurity. What powerful, horrible words! How did this lack of confidence all begin? No one wakes up one day and makes the conscious decision to be insecure about themselves! So HOW, WHEN, WHY did this all happen?

Insecurities come in so many different forms. For some it's body image; things like weight, physical appearance of our hands, feet, butts, breasts, and THIGHS! Others struggle with perceived emotional or intellectual deficiencies. Let's be honest, we beat ourselves up about so many things. We tell ourselves, "I'm not smart enough, not funny enough, too shy, too loud, too this, not enough that"...... The list is endless.

I have tried to remember where all the negativity began in my own life. When did I start beating myself up about my physical appearance, or my laugh or my scream? Yes, I said my "scream". You see, when the boys in grade school would chase us girls around the schoolyard, all the girls in my class would run from them with cute little Damsel in distress screams. Me, on the other hand, had what I would call a wounded bear kind of scream! As I ran from the boys, they turned and ran from me because of the shrieking HAHAHA! Maybe a bit of an exaggeration I know, but in my young mind that's how I perceived it.

For many of us, our insecurities cropped up at different stages in our lives. Personally, I can see it starting at a young age where, as kids we begin to notice differences in one another and begin verbalizing it to our friends.

It is sad to think how we compare ourselves to others. We constantly try to measure up to unrealistic expectations. We are inundated with social media, magazines, and television all sending false messages on how we should look, behave, parent and present ourselves to the world. With all the help from computers and technology now, anything is possible; we can make a carrot look like a beautiful woman in a bikini with just a few clicks of the mouse!

I was blessed with perfectly straight teeth. One would think this would be something to be proud of, but I can distinctly remember a girl in my class. Her name was Pamela (funny how those names never leave your memory...). She was one of the popular kids. She had braces, and not only did she have braces, but she had head gear. Seriously, HEADGEAR! Today that would have been dreadful, but back then, to me, Pamela was the cool kid! I wanted to have braces so badly so that I could be just like her. What was I thinking?! I even convinced my mom to take me to the dentist because I was bound and determined that I needed braces! I am sure the dentist thought I was absolutely insane!

But truth is, we constantly compare, everything about ourselves to others. Who says that the one we are comparing ourselves to is perfect? Who decides what perfect is anyway? And most likely, the very person we are trying to resemble, whether it be physically or otherwise, is probably trying to measure up to someone else too. It is a vicious cycle and it is time to break that cycle and choose to love ourselves the way God created us to be.

DAY 1 | Challenge

Today's Date: _____

1. Compile a list of your insecurities.
2. Record why it is that you feel uncomfortable about these things.
3. Write down where you believe these insecurities originated.
4. Copy today's "Truth to Stand On" and read it aloud to yourself 5 times but replace the word "I" with your name.

_____

_____

_____

_____

_____

_____

_____

Things I Learned About Myself Today.

Today's Date: _____

_____

_____

_____

_____

_____

_____

_____

_____

_____

_____

_____

_____

_____

_____

_____

_____

_____

_____

_____

DAY 2

Effects Of Our Insecurities

Effects Of Our Insecurities

Truth To Stand On:

We take every thought captive to make it obedient to Christ.
–2 Corinthians 10:5 (NIV)

As I look back through my personal journey on overcoming my insecurities, I can clearly see the effects that this negativity has had on my life and my relationships. Maybe you can relate.

As a young girl and growing in to my teens, I was constantly teased and made fun of for various reasons. My thighs for one. I am of German and Dutch descent. So I am, by no means, what people would call petite. Many times, upon entering a classroom, I would hear the comments, "WHOA… Is that an earthquake? Thunder Thighs is coming in the room." There were also other comments made referencing the fact that I have a very small breast size. AA to be exact. My daughters often ask if I'm sure that AA actually exists! Yes, I assure them it does! HAHAHA! My classmates felt the need to nickname me things such as "Carpenters Dream" because, as they would point out, I am flat as a board. I was also referred to as the President of the Itty Bitty T***y Committee. Lovely isn't it?! HAHAHA! But as silly and immature as all that seems, I took all that name-calling to heart and accepted it as truth. I believed that somehow, I was less-than because of these perceived deficiencies in my physical make-up.

I carried that all into my marriage. I felt like my body was not good enough for my husband and somehow, I would not be attractive enough for him. This led to struggles in the bedroom. Lights were never allowed to be on so that the "deficiencies" were not ever seen. Even though my husband continually assured me that he was quite aware of what I looked like, and that he loved me the way I was, I could only hear the lies in my head. "You're just not good enough".

How many times do we drag these insecurities, vulnerabilities and lies into our relationships with friends and spouses; feeling like we just don't measure up and therefore are not good enough?

When we feel inferior in any area of our lives, physical or otherwise, we become debilitated and don't function to our full potential. We are left feeling weak, inadequate and incapable of accomplishing great things! Relationships will not thrive and there will always be feelings of distrust and miscommunication.

God created us for GREATNESS! He created us in His image! (Gen 1:27) Ever hear the saying "I know I'm special because God doesn't make junk?" There is so much truth in that little old saying! We need to believe it!

The enemy, the devil, would love nothing more than for us to live lives that are not fulfilling our potential. And so, he puts these crazy thoughts and lies into our minds. When we feel weak and helpless, he has won the battle. Let's give the power back to the Lord and be victorious in our relationships and our lives, with God's power which is greater than anything the enemy can throw at us!

DAY 2 | Challenge

Today's Date: _____

1. Write down how your relationships with your spouse, friends, co-workers, children, etc. have been affected by your insecurities.
2. Brainstorm and record what changes you want to see happen in these relationships.
3. Repeat the "Truth to Stand On" to yourself 5 times replacing "We" with "I WILL".

_____

_____

_____

_____

_____

_____

_____

Things I Learned About Myself Today.

Today's Date: _____

_____

_____

_____

_____

_____

_____

_____

_____

_____

_____

_____

_____

_____

_____

_____

_____

_____

_____

_____

_____

_____

_____

DAY 3

Battle Of The Mind!

Battle Of The Mind!

Truth To Stand On:

You are a chosen people, a royal priesthood, a Holy nation, God's special possession, that you may declare the praises of Him who called you out of darkness into His wonderful light.
–1 Peter 2:9 (NIV)

Issues of insecurity are certainly a Battle of the Mind. We take on self-directed negativity or ideas that have been spoken into our hearts and minds by others to the point that we begin to accept it as truth. We lock it up in our brains where it grows like cancer and slowly it begins to distort our self-image.

The enemy knows our weaknesses and vulnerabilities and loves to attack and feast on those areas to bring us down.

I am not a great singer. In fact, I cannot hold a tune even if my life depended on it. That is not an insecurity for me, it is just plain fact. But, I LOVE to sing. I never allow that fact to stop me from singing out loud and freely..... um... well only while in the privacy of my own home when no one else is around, or in my car! HAHAHA! But here is a little story to show how the enemy knows our weaknesses and comes in to try to tear us down through our thought processes.

I was at a ladies' retreat enjoying the worship music and singing quite freely. In the middle of the service, all of a sudden, I had the thought, "Oh my goodness, the poor woman in front of me; she can hear me sing and she must be annoyed by my voice." I stopped worshiping. Then I thought, "You know, this is stupid! Why should I stop worshiping because I can't sing? I love to sing!" So, thinking I would beat the enemy at his own game, I decided to get out of my pew and stand in the isle so that no one was in front of me and I could sing freely and happily. Yes! Battle won! So, I thought...... but the devil is a sly old fox and he then proceeded to put negative thoughts into my friend's mind beside me. Do you see where this is going? She came to the retreat straight from the gym. She was running late and opted out of having a shower before she left the gym. As I moved out into the isle, she thought I had moved because she may have smelled bad from her workout. (Which by the way, was not the case!) She instantly stopped worshiping God freely for fear that raising her hands in worship would send the body odour further. Satan was victorious in that situation, sadly.

He knows our weaknesses and our areas of insecurities, and will stop at nothing to prevent us from being all that we can be for the betterment and development of the Lord's kingdom!

Yesterday, our "Truth to Stand On" verse was teaching us to take every thought captive. This is truly what we need to do. Anytime a thought comes into our mind, we need to stop and assess that thought and its purpose. Is this a thought that encourages life, or is this a thought that promotes destruction? If it is a thought of destruction and negativity we need to do away with it immediately. We need to speak positively to ourselves and about ourselves. This is referred to as positive self-talk and we should all seek to become experts on how to perform it.

I remember a video that went viral a few years ago of a young girl named Jessica. She was standing on her bathroom vanity talking to herself, telling herself all the things she liked. She mentioned things like her mom, her brother, her family, her dog, her hair and the list went on. I think we could certainly learn a lot from this little girl! We need to look at ourselves in the mirror, and I mean REALLY look down deep, beyond the surface and remind ourselves of our positive attributes. "Hey self, I am pretty GREAT!" Not in an arrogant way but in a loving way, with confidence in knowing we are heirs to the throne of God. We are children of the Most High God, and that the one who created this amazing earth is the one who created US! In doing this, we WILL be victorious in the battle of the mind and we will take control over our thought life!

Prayer For Today:

Lord, please continue to help me keep my mind pure before you. Help me to recognize the schemes of the enemy and how he will try to drown me in my thoughts. Thank you, Lord, that I am chosen by you! You love me unconditionally and you mean only good for my life!
Amen.

DAY 3 | Challenge

Today's Date: _____

1. Write down 5 things that you LIKE about yourself.
2. Look at yourself in the mirror and read those 5 things to yourself.
3. Write today's verse below with your name in it (personalize it).

_____

_____

_____

_____

_____

_____

_____

Things I Learned About Myself Today.

Today's Date: _____

_____

_____

_____

_____

_____

_____

_____

_____

_____

_____

_____

_____

_____

_____

_____

_____

_____

_____

_____

DAY 4

Fear

Fear

Truth To Stand On:

I sought the Lord, and He answered me. He delivered me from all my fears
–Psalms 34:4 (NIV)

Fear. The very word makes me feel uncomfortable. Fear or anxiety hinders our accomplishments and prevents our successes! There are so many different triggers to fear. Fear of heights, snakes, spiders, bears, public speaking, confined spaces or even butterflies. HAHAHA! Ya, that's a thing! My middle daughter, Vanessa, is afraid of butterflies. She may have gotten made fun of a time or two for that one! HAHAHA!

When we are insecure, our fears get in the way and have a way of taking over. Fear can become absolutely debilitating to us. God has a plan for each and every one of us! We all have gifts that He has created us to specifically move in. When we allow fear to set in, we are no longer allowing ourselves to flow in those gifting's or God-given talents. Not only do we miss out on the Lord's blessings, but others miss out as well.

I used to be horribly afraid to speak in public. Remember when we had to do speeches in school? They had to be 3 minutes long, be based on a specific topic, contain an introduction and a conclusion and all kinds of information in the middle. What purpose did this perceived torture fulfill? Amusement for the teacher I am sure! HAHAHA! I absolutely hated, hated, hated those times! I struggled so severely! I was so horribly insecure that the idea of standing front and centre of my class for them to look at me, and all of my flaws, was almost more than I could possibly bear! And then to have to fumble my way through a speech too?! If I could have run away to an undiscovered desert island, I would have relished the opportunity! Sounds dramatic, I know. But I am sure there is someone out there who can relate to my feelings! HAHAHA!

Speech day would arrive, and I would go to the front of the class and begin to speak. As I opened my mouth, all that would come out was my voice that was so high on adrenaline and fear that it sounded like I had just finished running a 25-km run. I couldn't catch my breath, and would begin to hyperventilate. Needless to say, the speech would end every time with the teacher giving me a cold cloth for my forehead and a brown paper bag to breathe into.

Excruciatingly painful, that is for sure! And now look at what I do for a living; I preach; every Sunday to my congregation, and then at conferences, retreats and camps to extremely large groups of people. God has a sense of humor, that is for sure! He took my weakness, my fear, my insecurities, and turned them into a blessing for His glory! All I needed to do was surrender my fear and anxiety to Him and He did the rest! It certainly wasn't easy in the beginning, but every time I stepped out in faith, the Lord never let me down. I could actually feel Him take over as I stood in faith, believing that this was His will for my life. Each time it got easier and easier. I still have a moment of nervousness each time I get up to speak. To me, it is simply a gentle reminder that I again, I need to completely rest in my Savior's arms. He so wants to do the same for you! What is your gifting that He has placed on your life? What is holding you back from sharing this gifting with others?

Take a moment and think about what a person might say on their deathbed. Chances are, you will never hear them say, "I wish I had a nicer car", "I wish I had more money", "I wish I would have been the CEO of a large company." NO! We hear people say, "I wish I would have spent more time with family", "I wish I would have travelled more", "I wish I would have stepped out of my box more", "I wish I would have shared my faith more"; all things that FEAR holds us back from. Don't live with regret! Push away fear and allow the Lord to move you, maybe even push you out of your box! Live in the confidence in knowing who you are in Him! And allow Him to flow through you to accomplish INCREDIBLE things for His glory!

DAY 4 | Challenge

Today's Date: _____

1. Think about and record what you think your God-given talents and gifts are.
2. Write out an active plan on how you can begin to use your gifts. (For example: Gift of Hospitality... Invite someone for dinner or lunch)
3. Make a list of 3 achievable things that you are fearful to do. Now, go do them and mark the date of when you did them on this page. Then go celebrate with someone close to you!

_____

_____

_____

_____

_____

_____

_____

_____

_____

_____

_____

_____

_____

_____

_____

_____

_____

_____

_____

_____

_____

_____

_____

_____

_____

_____

_____

_____

Things I Learned About Myself Today.

Today's Date: _____

_____

_____

_____

_____

_____

_____

_____

_____

_____

_____

_____

_____

_____

_____

_____

_____

_____

_____

_____

DAY 5

Living Each Day
With Expectation!

Living Each Day
With Expectation

Truth To Stand On:

Now to him who is able to do immeasurably more than all we ask or imagine, according to His power that is at work within us,
–Ephesians 3:20 (NIV)

Every day that the Lord gives us is a gift. I quite often say to people "any day above ground is a great day!" But let's take that one step further... any day above ground is a day we are still able to be effective for the kingdom and do great things for ourselves and others!

With that thought in the back of our minds, why not live a life of Expectation! We need to always expect something good to happen. Oftentimes when we are insecure, we tend to expect the worst. We find it very difficult to shift our thinking to more positive outcomes or expectations. When we are insecure we frequently look at others and see all they are accomplishing and feel that this will never happen for us because in our minds, we are lacking in one area or another and couldn't imagine good things happening in our lives. Oh, the power of negativity! But positivity has equal or greater power if we just practice it!

God does not pick favorites! He loves us all the same. He has blessings to pour out on everyone who seeks His face, not just a select few.
Sometimes in our insecurities we forget to dream and dream big.

I can remember as a kid in school always dreading when it came time for sports. First of all, I am not very athletic. I am, or should I say, I was a great long-distance runner in my younger days. But when it came to organized sports I was not great. I would become so stressed when it was time to pick teams; I knew that I would be the last to be chosen EVERY SINGLE TIME! I would stand there patiently waiting, hoping that all things would align, and I would be picked, at the very least, second last. Waiting and hearing all the names get called before mine, I would tell myself that I was obviously not good enough. Seriously, the pain and stress were unreal! Finally, my name would be reluctantly called, and everyone would scatter to their positions and the embarrassment of being left till last would slowly subside. How many of us can relate to this story?

Now the good news is, I am picked first by my Saviour I don't have to stand in the line-up, waiting, hoping to hear my name! I can live in the confidence in knowing that He not only created me to be how I am, but He picked me first What an amazing feeling! 2 Thessalonians 2:14 tells us that God chose us from the beginning! We are all His 1st choice. We aren't second best, 3rd best, we are #1 in His eyes. It does not get any better than that. With the Lord we don't sit on the sidelines waiting in anticipation that He is going to call us one day. NO! With Him we are first on His mind. It is simply up to us to accept that and take our place on His team. Look to Him with great expectation for great and wonderful things to happen. God knows every aspect of our being; He created us after-all. He even knows the amount of hairs on our head. Luke 12:7. He actually cares about us that much and takes that much interest in us that He knows every detail of our make-up. Now that has got to make you feel special! It certainly does me!

So, let's dream and dream BIG! Wake up and face each and every day with such colossal expectation that it allows God to do mighty and miraculous things in and through us! The sky is the limit!

DAY 5 | Challenge

Today's Date: _____

1. Write down a huge dream that you would love to achieve.
2. Tell someone close to you about your dream or post it on a social media site.
3. Pray for this dream to happen.
4. Save a space on this page to record the date that this dream it comes to fruition.
5. Write down your name and beside it "GOD CHOSE YOU FIRST"!!
6. Read that statement to yourself 5 times today.

_____

_____

_____

_____

_____

_____

Things I Learned About Myself Today.

Today's Date: _____

_____

_____

_____

_____

_____

_____

_____

_____

_____

_____

_____

_____

_____

_____

_____

_____

_____

_____

_____

DAY 6

We're With The Band

We're With The Band

Truth To Stand On:

"For I know the plans I have for you," declares the Lord, "plans to prosper you and not to harm you, plans to give you hope and a future."
–Jeremiah 29:11 (NIV)

"You like me, you really like me!" Some of you will remember this famous quote spoken by actress Sally Field during her acceptance speech at the Oscar's in 1984 for the movie "Places of the Heart". If you haven't seen it or you are way too young to remember, it is worth the YouTube search!

For a long time after its release, this declaration was the "tagline" that everyone would say to each other for fun. But looking back, I find it so interesting to watch this actress, who had been working in Hollywood for years and years, receive this award and just then come to the realization that people actually did like her! Many of us would think famous actresses and actors have it all together and think that they must be oozing with confidence. Many of us may even dream about being so confident and so self-assured. But in actuality, they too have moments of questioning their importance.

I can remember in high school I was on the "Dance Committee." We were responsible for hiring the bands that came in to entertain us for all the school dances. When the band would arrive, we were in charge of helping them set up and making sure they had water, and a meal before the dance. It was an instant backstage pass. Boy, did we feel like we were "All that and a bag of chips!" HAHAHA! As our classmates would begin to arrive for the dance, we were viewed as being pretty important, considering we were "with the band." Somehow having that title of dance committee and being in charge of the band, seemed to elevate our ranking with our friends. I guess at age 15, that is a pretty big deal. In reality though, being backstage with the band was not so glamorous; it was more work than being able to just enjoy the music and dance! Funny how that works. I was just a simple teenager looking for a place to belong and have some kind of rank that made me feel important!

Interestingly enough, many of us still feel the same way now, as I did as a young 15-year old; searching everywhere for that status. To say, "Hey, this is who I am!" We wanted something, anything, to give us a sense of importance. We find ourselves feeling empty and having no purpose in life. Some have described it to me as feeling invisible. Isn't that just like the enemy to put those thoughts and ideas into our minds and hearts?! We need to recognize our importance, not only to the Lord, but to the kingdom. We all have purpose in life.

When we are followers of Christ, we are promised a friend that will stick closer to us than a brother. We are promised blessings and all our needs to be met, and assurance to an eternity with Him; forgiveness of sin, peace in our lives… the list goes on and on. All we need to do is fall into His arms and trust in Him. There is no work, no bringing water to Him, no bringing meals to Him, no standing at the door as security for Him. He is there for all of us and loves us no matter what we have done or where we have come from. His love is uncondi-tional and is not determined by what we can offer Him.

You don't have to second-guess your importance or your status. Christ died on that cross for you; for forgiveness of your sins, for your freedom of all yokes of slavery! And the best part is… He would have done it even if you were the ONLY person on this earth! That's how much He loves you! And that is how important you are to Him. He sees you, knows all about you, and cares about every aspect of your life. You are not invisible to Him.

You have a backstage pass to the one who created this earth and who created you! Now that is a whole other level of cool, I would say!

DAY 6 | Challenge

Today's Date: _____

1. Copy Jeremiah 29:11 replacing the word "you" with your name.
2. Write down 3 or more ways that you are important to the kingdom.
3. You are an Oscar winner in God's eyes! Write out your acceptance speech to Him. Acknowledging all the ways you are important to Him and to those around you and thank the Lord for them!

_____

_____

_____

_____

_____

_____

_____

Things I Learned About Myself Today.

Today's Date: _____

_____

_____

_____

_____

_____

_____

_____

_____

_____

_____

_____

_____

_____

_____

_____

_____

_____

_____

_____

_____

DAY 7

Negative Vs Positive Thinking

Negative Vs Positive Thinking

Truth To Stand On:

For you created my innermost being: you knit me together in my mother's womb.
–Psalms 139:13 (NIV)

Someone once told me that I choose what to do with negative words spoken over me; I choose whether I would be hurt, or I choose whether I would just let it roll off my back. That thought process took me a bit of time to digest. Just being honest! HAHAHA! But it is certainly true. I am actually in control of my emotions and feelings. And I can decide whether to allow those words to have power over me or I have power over them.

How many times have we misunderstood someone and chosen to focus on perceived negativity, simply because that's our way of thinking? Positive thinking is so important!

There are many times when I send my husband a text and all I get back in reply is, "K". (and all the women out there are screaming... "YES!" HAHAHA!) It took me a long time to get over that. But to be honest, in the beginning, my brain would go to a whole other level. I would be upset and think he was mad at me or didn't have time to talk to me. Silliness, I know. But when we are in the habit of negative thinking that is what happens. We allow our imaginations to have the best of us. We need to steer away from negative thought processes and find positive in every situation.

I remember going 4 wheeling with some friends out in the bush. We were driving along and came upon a patch of pine trees that had been blown down during a storm. My girlfriend who was on a 4-wheeler in front of me yells out, "Smells like squished pine trees." I, on the other hand, trying my best to think positively in all situations, yell back at her, "Smells like Christmas!" I have never lived that one down, I must admit. It has become a standing joke; Wendy trying to be positive in all situations and sounding a bit cheesy at times in the process. But in all seriousness, in every situation, we can find something positive if we only try.

If negative words are spoken over you and they were intentionally negative, how can we get over that? We need to remember that we are in charge of our emotions and our thoughts. So, the words spoken were that person's thoughts, not yours. We need to come to a place in our minds that we know who we are and what we believe to be true about ourselves and be confident in that. We will never ever make every single person happy. Oh, how that pains me at times! Yes, I am a people pleaser and want everyone to love me all the time. But, I also need to realize that I will never make everyone happy. Some people actually get irritated by me. For some, I'm too happy, laugh too loud, am too energetic, etc. But we are not focusing on negativity, right? HAHAHA! I need to know that, yes, it's true, I am a happy person; yes, I laugh loudly; yes, I have a lot of energy and not everyone is like that. But the fact is, this is who I am, I can't change those things, nor should I want to. If people choose to point out those facts, then that's OK. But I choose whether I am going to let it bother me or not.

Choose today positive thinking and stay clear of negative thoughts. Be who God created you to be. The world would be pretty boring if we were all the same! Diversity is what makes this world so interesting!

And remember, sometimes the person you are texting just doesn't have time to write a whole message and assumes that "K" is sufficient. That's who they are; maybe a little less chatty than we may be, but that's OK.

DAY 7 | Challenge

Today's Date: _____

1. Write down 3 positive things about who you are.
   Send 3 people a note or a message today pointing out something
2. positive you see in them. (Spread the love!)
3. Write down on this page this promise, "I promise to think positively in all situations", and sign it!

_____

_____

_____

_____

_____

_____

_____

Things I Learned About Myself Today.

Today's Date: _____

_____
_____
_____
_____
_____
_____
_____
_____
_____
_____
_____
_____
_____
_____
_____
_____
_____
_____
_____
_____

DAY 8

You Are Royalty!

You Are Royalty!

Truth To Stand On:

But you are a chosen people. A royal priesthood, a holy nation, God's special possession, that you may declare the praises of Him who called you out of darkness into His wonderful light.
–1 Peter 2:9 (NIV)

There has been great interest in ancestry in recent years. People want to discover their roots and be able to trace their lineage. Using DNA and other methods they are now able to track down what country their ancestors really came from. Interestingly enough, I have found many people who were actually disappointed when they found out. I guess being told for so many years that you are of particular descent, only to find out in actuality you are from somewhere else, can be a little disconcerting, or even disappointing.

My mom was born in Holland and moved to Canada when she was 12. My dad was born in Germany and moved to Canada when he was 19. So, I have a very European background. This is what I blame my physical stature on, by the way! HAHA! It's a physique that I have now grown to love and appreciate.

The area my dad came from is very close to the France border. And there were a few times during the 2 World Wars that this part of Germany was taken over by France. When my dad came to Canada the 1st time his passport was actually issued from France. In the time he was here in Canada, authority had returned to Germany. Talk about not knowing who you are! One minute he was French, the next he was back to German. This caused a lot of problems when he did go home for a visit because no one knew what to do with him; A man without a country. I'm reminded of the movie, "The Terminal" starring Tom Hanks.

Apparently, as family history would have it, I had a great, great uncle that was born in France and escaped into Germany in a manure truck during the war. And that is how my family began their lives in Germany. Now there is a story you can be proud of. HAHA!

I have never done my DNA or researched my ancestry. I am sure it would be very interesting to see how we all came to be where we are. With the little knowledge that I do have, I am happy to say that I am part German and part Dutch with some French in the mix somewhere. My extended family is from Germany and Holland and I count it a huge blessing to have such incredible relationships with them. I am still very much in touch with them now and I enjoy seeing those ties continue with my children as well. I never ever want to forget our roots.

What I am most proud of though is, although I am of German and Dutch descent physically, I am of royal blood as well! Royalty from my Saviour, God Most High! Yes, when we have Christ in our lives, we are all heirs to our Heavenly Father. It is God who created us. And it is His DNA that flows through our bodies. This is one DNA test and family tree no one could be disappointed in discovering.

It is my personal goal to live and be as much like Him as I can possibly be. That way when people look at me, they not only see me, but they see my Heavenly Father in me as well.

If you have Christ in your life, we share the same DNA! We are all royalty! God is our Heavenly Father and He cares about all of us just the same! You can search out more about your family history by getting into the word of God, and you don't even have to send your spit to someone at a lab to be tested! You can have this assurance in your heart of who you are and where you came from simply by surrendering your life to Him.

DAY 8 | Challenge

Today's Date: _____

1.   Write out today's "To Stand On" but replace "you" with "I/me".
2.   Write yourself a letter indicating that your DNA results just came in and that you are from Royal descent! How Very Exciting!

_____

_____

_____

_____

_____

_____

_____

Things I Learned About Myself Today.

Today's Date: _____

_____

_____

_____

_____

_____

_____

_____

_____

_____

_____

_____

_____

_____

_____

_____

_____

_____

_____

_____

DAY 9

Not Everything Is As It Seems

Not Everything Is As It Seems

Truth To Stand On:

I can do all things through Christ who gives me strength.
–Philippians 4:13 (NIV)

Today I start off this devotional to simply admit... "I am a Facebook Addict"! Yes, there it is out in the open! I feel a sense of relief radiating from my spirit as I share that with all of you! HAHAHA!

So many people oppose social media. I have to say, I agree to a point, but there are positive aspects of it as well. I love social media because it helps me to connect with family members who are oceans away. It also has become a place where ministry often happens, and I am able to pour into people's lives. I also just love the entertainment of it all!

On the negative side though, it certainly can give us false ideas and thoughts about other people's lives. We certainly can't believe everything we see. Hopefully that doesn't come as a shock to any of you! HAHAHA!

There is a story of a Dutch girl who in 2014 took a 5-week tour to south east Asia. Or so she said! She was doing an experiment for an assignment at school. How could she fake this trip and make it look like she actually went away using social media? With only her boyfriend in on the ruse, she began her journey convincing all family and friends that she was on an incredible journey touring the beautiful sites of Asia. She was able to turn her apartment into what looked like a hotel room where she Skyped with people "back home" to share her adventures with. She posted pictures and very carefully Photoshopped herself in the photos. All was very convincing and authentic-looking. Everyone was convinced and never thought any different.

When she was done her 5-week supposed journey, she sat her family down to tell them what she had done. They were all shocked as you can imagine. It became a huge story all over the news that she was able to pull off such a feat; all to prove how our lives on social media certainly are not always what they seem to be.

Some of you may be shocked; some of you may think that was cruel and unfair; some of you, like me, may even think, "Wow! I would love to try that. Wouldn't it be funny?! HAHA! But in a sense, we have all probably pulled off a similar stunt a time or two. Not with intentions to shock family, but possibly with the intent to show how wonderful our lives actually are. How have we done this you ask?

I'm sure many of us have gone to a park with our children and taken 1000 pictures of our kids playing on the monkey bars, swinging on the swings, and playing in the sand. Out of those 1000 pictures 998 of them capture a child crying, screaming, pulling the hair of a sibling, or worse! But we have 2 wonderful, incredible pictures where yes, they are actually looking happy and smiling! And what do we do? We post those 2 pictures, delete the other 998 and entitle our post "Great Day At The Park With The Kids Today!" HAHAHA! All the while we are heading home promising ourselves that we will never go to the park again because it causes so much stress in our lives, and how can you children not get along with your siblings is beyond me! HAHA! We are all guilty. We love to show the perfect moments to the public but not often admit our faults. Why? For fear of what others may think.

The sad part of this is all the other moms who took their kids to the park, and later looked on Facebook, are asking themselves why their kids aren't like everyone else's perfect and well-behaved children.

Now with filters and editing programs we can make our pictures change from dull and ordinary to beautiful pieces of art. Or so my adult kids tell me anyway! I still have not conquered the art of editing photos I must admit. Check out my Instagram page, you will see what I mean. (Boring!) HAHA!

I write all of this to simply say, we are all the same! We all struggle with life from time to time. What looks like perfect lives on social media is not always true. I bet if you posted a picture of your child's messy bedroom or your messy kitchen with dishes stacked to the ceiling and said, "This Is Real Life", you will get so many responses of people saying… "Yes, yes, yes, it is! Thank you for sharing!" HAHA! Try it and see!

Let's be honest, we have all questioned ourselves; if we are good parents, if we are good housekeepers, if we are providing healthy enough meals for our families, should I be gluten free like other moms, or maybe vegan. No offence to those who are, I love the discipline it takes to do that. I, on the other hand, just love a good cheeseburger from time to time and finish it off with a Reese peanut butter cup! Do I do that daily? No, of course not. Sometimes I wash the cheeseburger down with a carrot stick! (kidding!) In all seriousness though, who are we to judge others? We are all human and we all make mistakes. We all are doing the best we can. Let's live confidently with the knowledge that we are doing our best, and stop comparing ourselves to other people. Do we really know what goes on behind closed doors of each person's home? No, of course not. Do we need to know? Of course not! So, in saying all that, let's live our lives asking the Lord to lead and guide us and feel confident in the fact that we are doing the best job we can do!

In the book of Psalms 143:10 David makes a request of the Lord. He asks the Lord to teach him God's will for his life and help to keep him on level ground. I find this interesting that he asks to be kept on "level ground". He knows in life we can have ups and downs, and he is requesting God to help him stay on a good path. Life is no different from back then as it is now, in that sense. We still require the help of our Heavenly Father to teach, lead, and guide us through whatever trials life will bring us. Surrender all your worries and cares upon Him. He will indeed help you through!

DAY 9 | Challenge

Today's Date: _____

1. Take a picture of a messy room within your home, (kitchen, bedroom, or living room). Post it on Facebook and title it, "This is real life... anyone agree?" Record the comments here.
2. Find a mom with young children, (someone you know or someone you see in a store). Give them an encouraging word to tell them they are doing a great job!
3. Now tell yourself the same message! Write it here and end it off with the "Truth to Stand On" verse.

_____

_____

_____

_____

_____

_____

Things I Learned About Myself Today.

Today's Date: _____

_____

_____

_____

_____

_____

_____

_____

_____

_____

_____

_____

_____

_____

_____

_____

_____

_____

_____

_____

DAY 10

———

Thank Goodness
You Can't Read My Mind

Thank Goodness
You Can't Read My Mind

Truth To Stand On:

Do not let anyone look down on you because you are young, but set an example for the believers in speech, in conduct, in love, in faith, and in purity.
–1 Timothy 4:12 (NIV)

I think it is safe to say we all know that everyone, at some point has struggled with some sort of insecurity. But what we don't all realize is that we don't all show our insecurities. In most cases no one can actually tell we are insecure unless we make it known. Hence the reason why we feel like we are the only ones who feel this way.

A few years ago, I was invited to an "Invitation Only" leadership retreat. It was an honor to be invited and included in this very incredible experience. I must admit though, the insecure part of my brain kicked in. Why was I invited? Who am I to be considered important enough to be amongst all these other leaders, etc.

In the days leading up to the retreat I had carefully planned out my wardrobe and what hairstyles I would wear each day. (Yes this is what some women do, for any men who may be reading this HAHA!). Upon arriving to the first session, as I was about to walk into the room the tornado started in my stomach. Would there be anyone there I knew? Where would I sit? Would I be the only person taking notes on paper instead of a laptop or a tablet? Yes, silly I know, but just being honest.

As I approached the room, I shot up a quick prayer to the Lord. "Lord, help me to represent the leader you have called me to be." And I walked in. Thankfully I knew one person, who happened to be part of the attendee selection group. I quickly walked over and struck up a conversation with him. I began as confidently as I could muster, to express my appreciation to be invited to this event. Conversation went well, and I was feeling good until the room began to fill with many male leaders that I have never met nor seen before in my life. Many of them knew each other and began to laugh and chat and share inside jokes together. Awkward! But I remained confident, as best as I could, in my calling and chose to not let anyone see or know what was going on inside my head.

Finally, one other woman walked in. I smiled at her and assumed she was probably feeling the same way as me. I went to grab a chair and looked at her as to invite her to sit beside me. She came, and we struck up a great conversation, getting to know each other. We discussed where we were in ministry, shared family stories, spoke of children, husbands etc. I made a new friend! What a blessing! I could breathe again! Class began. It turned out to be an incredible learning experience and I went away feeling included, challenged, and stretched in my ministry skills.

Many months later, my new friend and I continued our friendship and kept in contact. We met for dinner one evening when I was in her area. We began to chat about the retreat and how much we learned over the course of those few days. I then began to tell her openly how nervous I was in the beginning. I told her about my stomach doing somersaults, and how I felt like I would pass out. She was "shocked", in her words. She didn't believe me at all. I, on the other hand, was stunned at her response to my confession. "Seriously?!" I said. I felt like it was all over my face; every single insecurity, every doubt, everything. "Not at all," she replied. In fact, she continued, "I was looking at you and as soon as I saw you, I thought, 'wow, there is a leader!'".

I could not believe what I was hearing. I sat in awe of her words. Then I remembered my little prayer. "Lord, help me to be the leader you have called me to be". I went into that room not with a confidence of my own, but with a confidence God gave me. Inside I was dying. But guess what? No one can read my mind! Even though I felt insignificant amongst all those other leaders, I was leaning on the Lord completely. He gave me the covering I needed and no one was any wiser.

So, what does this tell me? "Fake it till you make it", I guess. HAHA! Not that I was being a fake, of course not. But, even though I didn't feel confident in my leadership abilities I chose to walk in the confidence of what the Lord saw in me. Sometimes we need to just choose to walk in what God sees, putting our thoughts aside and allowing His thoughts to be stronger. Until such point that we begin to actually see what He sees in us.

In the scripture verse Romans 12:2 it encourages us to allow God to transform our minds. We need to give God permission to do just that. To change the way we think about everything, especially the way we think about ourselves. He sees us as these wonderful creations who have potential to accomplish so much in our lives. If we listen to His voice and His way of thinking, we will eventually start to see exactly what He sees in us. Renew your mind. It's like putting your mind and your thoughts about yourself into a washing machine and coming out refreshed and renewed!

DAY 10 | Challenge

Today's Date: _____

1. Only one challenge today because it's a biggie! Ready, Set, GO.....
   Do something completely out of your box. If you are uncomfortable to have people into your home for dinner, plan a dinner party. If you are uncomfortable shaking hands at church, make yourself get out of the pew, go to the opposite side of the room and shake someone's hand. If there is an outfit you have in your closet you haven't worn for fear of what others will think, put it on and wear it to your next church service or outing somewhere. Everyone's fears are different. What's yours? Today is the day we choose to face them. Even if you don't feel confident inside, walk in the confidence the Lord has for you. Pray, asking Him to go with you and then GO.....
   Record here everything that happened. What you did, how it went, how you felt before and after. And then answer this question; Did anyone really know you were insecure about doing what you did?

   _____

   _____

   _____

Things I Learned About Myself Today.

Today's Date: _____

_____

_____

_____

_____

_____

_____

_____

_____

_____

_____

_____

_____

_____

_____

_____

_____

_____

DAY 11

Me Time

Me Time

Truth To Stand On:

But Jesus often withdrew to lonely places and prayed.
–Luke 5:16 (NIV)

How many of us have ever experienced the feeling of guilt for taking time for just us? And the crowd goes wild in agreement! Right! Why is that? Why do we feel like it is bad for us to take time to do something just for us?

I am not only a Pastor, but a mom, and a part time hair stylist. My life is continually inundated with people who need a piece of me. I wear different hats throughout each day. I am either being a mom and giving advice, motherly love and encouragement; or a hair stylist who is helping people to feel better about themselves with a new style; or I am a pastor who is planning the next sermon that will speak to my congregation, helping my people through issues in their lives, or planning church and community outreach events.

I have to say I absolutely love, love, love what I do each and every day. I know beyond a shadow of a doubt, I am doing exactly what God has called me to do and I truly get excited to say, "This is what I GET to do!" I feel that much love and passion for each of the hats that I wear.

In saying all of that, I still need to refuel my tank on a regular basis. How can I accomplish all that is required of me if I continually give out and forget to fill back up? How can I find joy in what I do if I am tired and run down and resentful because all my time is spent meeting the needs of others.

Many of us get burnt out by giving, giving, giving, until there is nothing left of us to give. We slowly begin to forget who we are and who we were created to be. Somehow, we lose sight of what our hopes and dreams are because we were so busy helping others find theirs.

So here it is everyone, permission to do something just for YOU!

As I write this book, I am 25 lbs slimmer than I was 4 months ago. I still have about another 35lb to go. No, I am not looking to be a size 2, I simply want to be a healthier version of myself. Truth be known, I have a horrible family history of heart disease. And that dreaded belly fat has simply got to go if I want to remain breathing and effective for the Kingdom on this earth past age 55. In my family that is the age where many of my aunts and uncles have sadly left us because of heart attacks and heart related issues. I plan to beat the odds!

So, to accomplish this, I have decided to not only change my eating habits, but to allow myself to have 1 hour 6 days a week to exercise as well. I shut my phone off and go do my thing. It is the best 1 hour that I get to do something just for me. It is me-time. And I don't feel guilty at all.

This me-time not only helps me in my weight loss efforts, it also revitalizes my brain. Because this is something I truly enjoy doing. Yes, I am one of the few who actually truly enjoys working out. It gives me an adrenaline rush and I feel so great afterwards.

Exercising, doing a bike tour, hiking; all of these activities are things that bring pleasure to me. What brings pleasure to you? What activity or hobby do you enjoy that you have set on the back burner because you have so many others needs to take care of?

It's time to figure out who you are again. When we forget who we are and lose sight of that, the insecurities take over and the resentment towards others for taking up all your time can be overwhelming. Take some time to find you again. And give yourself permission to enjoy those things that you previously enjoyed again. Your house will continually need cleaning no matter how much time spend on it, laundry will never go away, garages will always be in need of organizing and lawns will always need to be cut. These are things that are just part of life. We can spend so much time and effort on the tasks of life, just going through the motions and never really doing things that bring us pure JOY!

When we lose our dreams, lose our enjoyment and excitement for life, we lose ourselves. No one wants to wake up at age 89 and think, "I never accomplished my dream!"

Kids will grow up and move out, jobs will come and go, it is time to find your identity again!

It's time to get rid of the feeling of guilt. Even Jesus took time away to pray, rest and relax. He is our example of how we are to live our lives. If He finds it important enough to do it guilt free, why would we think any different.

Jesus was constantly meeting the needs of others. He knew the importance of refueling. It is recorded in the scripture for a reason; so that we would learn that it is OK for us to do the same.

Kick those feelings of guilt to the curb and find time for YOU! I know for some that will be a challenge. Look at your schedule for the day. Find even 10 minutes to do something that is just for you. It may mean getting up a little earlier than normal, it may even mean you have to say the dreaded word, "No" to someone. But allow yourself to do that. Jesus did! So should we!

P.S. I'll let you know at the end of this book if I accomplished the last 35lbs! Be cheering me on please! HAHA!

DAY 11 | Challenge

Today's Date: _____

1. Take some time to think about what makes you happy. What would your perfect me-time look like? Write that down here.
2. Look at your day and figure out at what point in the day you could carve out enough time to have some me-time.
3. Set yourself a reminder on your phone or your day timer that you have a "daily appointment" with yourself for some much needed me-time!
4. Find an accountability partner who will check on you once in awhile to make sure you are sticking to your guilt-free me-time.
5. Have your accountability partner read this part of your journal and sign on the bottom of this page that they will keep you accountable.

_____

_____

_____

_____

_____

Things I Learned About Myself Today.

Today's Date: _____

_____

_____

_____

_____

_____

_____

_____

_____

_____

_____

_____

_____

_____

_____

_____

_____

_____

_____

_____

DAY 12

No Bad Days

No Bad Days

Truth To Stand On:

Having hope will give you courage, you will be protected and will rest in safety. You will lie down unafraid, and many will look to you for help
–Job 11:18-19 (NIV)

Many years ago, my husband and I were part of a Fitness Franchise. My husband was hired as the Canadian sales rep and I was hired as a "Mentor". My job was to travel around Canada helping new owners open their clubs and then mentor them throughout their first week of opening and training staff.
Each year we had a huge convention to attend with all franchise owners and their staff from the USA and Canada together. This was a huge event with the main purpose to inspire owners and staff to continue being successful in their business.

The most memorable speaker that I recall from all the events I attended was a man by the name of Zig Ziglar. The title of his speech was called "No Bad Days". It has stuck with me ever since. In his speech he encouraged all of us that really, there should never be a bad day. He said that somewhere in this world, somewhere, somehow there is someone, who is having a worse day then we are. He didn't mean it to negate the fact that sometimes we have bad things happen to us, but to encourage us that things can always be worse. He also talked about finding the good in all things, and being thankful for them.

In those moments when I get down on myself for silly things, I often think about his words. Somewhere in this world there is a mom who has lost a child to illness, a family whose dad lost his job and now they have no idea how their heating bill will be paid, or someone just received news that they have cancer. How can I complain because of something that I don't like about myself or about my life?

We read about the Israelites in the bible, who constantly complained to Moses about so many things. They were sick of eating manna all the time, then too much quail. They constantly dreamed about how much better their lives were back in Egypt. It is easy for us to criticize them for their constant grumbling and complaining. But in a lot of ways, aren't we oftentimes, a lot like them? We complain about silly things as well. But if we took a moment to stand back and truly see how blessed we are, we may just be shocked.

Our lives are all about perspective. We can look at what we don't have and wish we had something different, or we could choose to feel blessed and happy with what we do have.

In the book of Luke, we read a story about an extremely poor widow putting her offering in at church. She gave two mites, which in those days, was a very small amount. The issue here is not so much the amount she gave, but the fact that she gave. She gave sacrificially of the meagre amount of money she made in a month. Nowhere do we read that she was upset with God because of her lifestyle, or that she complained at all about her situation. She gave what she had in faith that it would be used for the glory of the Lord, plain and simple. Jesus made it clear to his disciples that she gave, in essence, more than anyone else who gave huge amounts of money. Why? Because she gave what she had.

My question to us is, what do we give? God has blessed us all with gifts, abilities, and much potential to use for His glory. Do we use it? Or do we complain because it just isn't as good as we think it should be.

This widow woman gave of what she had. So should we.
Let's choose to get up each and every day happy to be breathing, and excited for how God can use us that day! If He can use a widow's mite to accomplish much for His glory, imagine with me for a moment what He could use our offering for. I don't necessarily mean financial offering, but I mean our offering of our lives and our positive attitudes towards life.

I want to be seen by others as someone who has contagious happiness. Yes, I understand that bad things happen in life.

We can't always live on the mountain top. But we can choose to take on a positive perspective and find hope in all situations through our faith in Jesus Christ, just as our widow friend.

As Zig says, "No bad days!"

DAY 12 | Challenge

Today's Date: _____

This challenge will actually last for one full week (Longer if you are brave! HAHA!).

1. Find yourself an elastic band or a rubber bracelet or some sort of bracelet that you can move from one wrist to the other easily.
2. Check which arm you begin this challenge on. Left___ Right___
   For 7 days you are to, very carefully, be aware of your thoughts and the words that come from your mouth. Each time a complaint or negative word comes into your mind or out of your mouth you need to switch the bracelet to the other wrist. On this sheet you are to keep track of what your thoughts and complaints were. At the end of the week you must write yourself a letter to process if those complaints were really worth the complaints.

   READY, SET, GO...................

   Date Started: _____

Day 1 Thoughts/ How many times bracelet was switched?:

_____

_____

_____

_____

_____

Day 2 Thoughts/ How many times bracelet was switched?:

_____

_____

_____

_____

_____

Day 3 Thoughts/ How many times bracelet was switched?:

_____

_____

_____

_____

_____

Day 4 Thoughts/ How many times bracelet was switched?:

_____

_____

_____

_____

_____

Day 5 Thoughts/ How many times bracelet was switched?:

_____

_____

_____

_____

_____

Day 6 Thoughts/ How many times bracelet was switched?:

_____

_____

_____

_____

_____

Day 7 Thoughts/ How many times bracelet was switched?:

_____

_____

_____

_____

_____

Date Started: _____

Things I Learned About Myself Today.

Today's Date: _____

_____

_____

_____

_____

_____

_____

_____

_____

_____

_____

_____

_____

_____

_____

_____

_____

_____

_____

_____

_____

_____

DAY 13

For Such A Time As This

For Such A Time As This

Truth To Stand On:

Now then, stand still and see this great thing the Lord is about to do before your eyes!
–1 Samuel 12:16 (NIV)

This morning as I was sitting watching the news while drinking my healthy protein shake, (yes, still on the weight loss plan. HAHA!) I found myself overwhelmed with all that is taking place in the world. It seems there is tragedy after tragedy; from hurricanes wiping out multiple countries all in one sweep to random shootings happening in places that really should be safe havens for people. All this sadness and grief could really bring us down and cause us to wonder, where is God in all this. And then God reminded me, not only is He still here and very much alive, but He has chosen us as believers, and equipped us to be the ones to bring light to the darkness.

Think about the story in the Old Testament of Esther. When I read her story I really get a sense that she is like so many of us. Looking at our lives and thinking "oh we are so insignificant; how could we possibly change the world around us?". Esther was an orphan girl who was taken by no choice of her own to be brought to a King to see if he wanted her as his wife. She was among thousands of other girls. The chances of her winning the King's heart would be about the same odds as we have of winning the lottery. (Which I don't play, so I guess my odds are really low!! HAHA!). But God had a plan.

This simple orphan girl who seemed insignificant to most had a special calling and purpose on her life. God divinely placed her in that kingdom for His Kingdom's purposes. Esther became Queen! (I have more to tell you about that process in Day 14). Not too long after her being crowned Queen it was man, was scheming to have all Jews annihilated. Mordecai, Esther's cousin who took care of her as she grew up, encouraged her that maybe she was placed in this kingdom for such a time as this! When we read this story, Esther wasn't too thrilled with the idea at first, as many of us would relate, I'm sure.

I am sure that she felt the same way I did today as I sat watching the news. Thoughts like, "This is too big for me to have an impact, how can I possibly bring any good into this situation?" She must have felt helpless. Sometimes the situation seems too difficult for us to be able to help in any way. So, we back away in the hopes that someone else will step up to the plate.

After much convincing by Mordecai, Esther finally decided to trust in the Lord, and do what she could do. She chose to step out of what she thought her capabilities were and trust that God was bigger. She even made the statement that "if I perish, I perish". That's HUGE!

God rewarded her boldness and a whole Jewish nation was saved because of her willingness to step out of her thoughts of insecurities and put her whole trust in the Lord. Incredible!

What is it that God could do through you if you were willing to put your feelings of insecurity aside and allow Him to flow through you in power and might?! God was able to save a whole nation because of Esther. Often, we read about bible characters and think that they were so much greater than all of us. This is not the case. She was a simple orphan girl. No special degrees, no special training, nothing. She merely trusted in God and put her thoughts aside and allowed God to do all the work. And did He ever!

In our world today, there is so much darkness; so many people who are feeling lonely, helpless and hopeless. We have the Lord in our hearts. We know and have seen His power. It is time for us to step out of our insecurities and what we think we know about ourselves and allow the Lord to work through us to save nations from evil.

God is calling out to all of us saying, "Please! For such a time as this!"

Sometimes we allow our insecurities to stop us from being effective for the Kingdom. If Esther would have argued with her cousin Mordecai, and said, "Don't you know, I'm not able to do that", or "I'm too scared", or "That is just way out of my comfort zone". What would have happened? Maybe God would have called another to save the nation, true. But would you really want to be the one who missed out on the chance for God to use you in such an incredible way? I don't know about you, but I never want to be the one who misses out on having that incredible opportunity.

Let's all choose to be like Esther. Breaking out of what we know in our human minds and allowing our creator God to pour out His power through us to accomplish greatness! There is no room for insecurities in God's plan. All He requires of us is a willing and surrendered heart. He will take care of the rest. He will equip us with all we need, we just merely need to show up!

DAY 10 | Challenge

Today's Date: _____

1. Think of 3 people that you know who are shut-ins, lonely, hurting or just in need of an encouraging word. Pray about how you could be a blessing to them in a practical way and bring a bit of light into their lives!

2. Make a plan. Go be a blessing to them. ("For Such a Time as This!") Ideas: Bring a Tim Horton's Coffee to someone and have a visit, bake some cookies and deliver them, read scripture to someone in a hospital, buy flowers and deliver them, babysit for a young mom, show up to someone's home and do their dishes for them.

3. Record here what you did and how it felt to be the one God used for greatness.

_____

_____

_____

_____

_____

Things I Learned About Myself Today.

Today's Date: _____

_____

_____

_____

_____

_____

_____

_____

_____

_____

_____

_____

_____

_____

_____

_____

_____

_____

DAY 14

Not My Will, But Yours Lord!

DAY
14

Not My Will, But Yours Lord!

Truth To Stand On:

So do not fear, for I am with you; do not be dismayed, for I am your God. I will strengthen you and help you, I will uphold you with my righteousness right hand.
–Isaiah 41:10 (NIV)

Yesterday's devotional was a challenge for you to choose to be used by the Lord for greatness for such a time as this. I would like to continue looking at the story of Esther and dig just a little deeper into her story.

When we allow our insecurities to get the best of us, we are in a sense telling the Lord that we will choose how we will live our lives and will not surrender fully to His will. It is almost like saying that we don't fully trust Him. As I study Esther's story I see an interesting part that often gets over-looked; her incredible willingness to put aside her will for the sake of the kingdom.

Esther was brought into the palace as a potential bride to King Xerxes. She, along with thousands of other girls, all had one opportunity to stand out more than the others and win the king's heart for position of Queen over Persia.

For one year prior to her evening with the king, all the girls were sent to what would be known today as a spa to prepare fully for this grand event. Imagine, spa treatments for one year! "Sign me up PLEASE!" Says all women everywhere! After the one-year process of milk baths and soaking in expensive perfumes, all the girls were informed that anything they chose to wear on their night with king Xerxes would be theirs to keep even if they weren't chosen by him. They could wear any gown they chose, any jewelry, any perfume, they could do their hair how they wanted, everything was completely up to them. Each night these young maidens would

LLORD Why Are My THIGHS Not Like HERS??

enter the king's private quarters hoping to be the one to steal his heart. Girl after girl was rejected.

And then the night came; it was now Esther's turn. Esther was different. She went to the one person who was closest to the king, the one who knew him best and asked advice on what the king would like best. She probably asked questions like, "What is the king's favourite perfume?", "What is the king's favourite colour?", "How should I wear my hair?", "What would make him happy?"
She did not enter the throne room of the king wearing what she thought was best, but she put on what she knew her king would like best. Because she chose his will and desire over her own she was able to win the king's heart and be given the title of Queen.

What does this say to you as you hear this story? I look at this and think this is how I should enter the throne room of the Lord, my King. I should talk to Jesus, the one who knows Him best and find out what does my King, my creator, want for my life? How should I present myself to Him? What is the aroma that makes Him happy? What is the lifestyle that would make Him happy? What is it about my life that will please my King? I need to surrender all my thoughts of what I think my life should look like and what I think I can do for the Kingdom and let His will be done. I need to find out what makes Him happy and in turn please Him with my actions.

When we do things all on our own, without seeking the one who knows the King best, we miss out on the greater prize! I don't know about you, but I never want to miss out on the prize God has for me!

What may be stopping you from setting your will aside and following the will of the King? Is it fear of the unknown, fear of being hurt or rejected, or fear of failing?

The Lord is here to love and support you. He promises to never let you go. He will never leave you nor forsake you. (Heb 13:5). God will never ask you to do something that he does not think you are able to do. He will always equip and prepare you. All you need to do is surrender! Are you ready?

DAY 14 | Challenge

Today's Date: _____

1. Make a list here of all the ways that you may be subconsciously holding back from the Lord; not submitting your complete will to Him.
2. Write Him a letter of submission. Tell Him you are going to allow Him to take over all those areas you have been holding onto.
3. Sign the bottom of your letter as a declaration that you are committed to this new way of living.

_____

_____

_____

_____

_____

_____

_____

Things I Learned About Myself Today.

Today's Date: _____

_____

_____

_____

_____

_____

_____

_____

_____

_____

_____

_____

_____

_____

_____

_____

_____

_____

_____

_____

DAY 15

I Hate New Year's Resolutions

I Hate New Year's Resolutions

Truth To Stand On:

Brothers and sisters, I do not consider myself yet to have taken hold of it. But one thing I do: Forgetting what is behind and straining toward what is ahead, I press on toward the goal to win the prize for which God has called me heavenward in Christ Jesus.
–Philippians 3:13-14 (NIV)

As I write today's devotional it is the beginning of November. Halloween is over and now the buzz of Christmas is in the air. My apologies to those who are reading this in the middle of summer! HAHA! I'm sure you really want to be thinking about Christmas while you're soaking up the sun in the middle of July! HAHA!

Very quickly after Christmas comes New Years Eve! How many of us make New Year's resolutions? Oh, if I had a dime for every broken New Year's resolution ever made in my lifetime I'd be rich! HAHA! Who really ever sticks to them? Maybe less than 1% I am sure. Why do we put ourselves through the torture of that year after year. I think I read somewhere that New Year's resolutions are broken generally before February rolls around; which means we tend to last maybe a month if we are lucky.

I always have to chuckle at the commercials on television that air in the new year. It is all about weight loss, diet programs and exercise videos. We are inundated everywhere with new, sure-fire ways to get fit and actually stick to the #1 New Year's resolution, which is weight loss. Oh, these companies and their marketing teams know us so well! As I told you before, my husband and I were involved in a fitness franchise years ago and I can attest to this fact. I spent many a meeting focusing on making plans to get the word out about our franchise, strategically after the eat-fest of Christmas, but before the New Year hits.

I am proud to say, I have finally, after many failed attempts, decided to no longer make a New Year's resolution. In its place I have chosen a much wiser approach to the New Year. Over the past number of years, I have decided to take a long hard look at the events of my life from the previous year, and then I have decided to challenge myself to be better in the next year in certain areas.

So, in saying this, things I would look at are, how did I affect my community for the Kingdom? How did I use my talents and gifts for God's glory? Did I grow personally in my walk with Him, into a deeper relationship or did I stay stagnant? Did I push myself further out of the box then I did last year? Was I willing to go places or do things that I maybe would not have done before? Am I a better person now than I was at the start of the New Year last year?

I find this kind of thinking to be a lot more effective than making a resolution that I know I will not stick to.

Taking time to re-examine yourself and reflect on your life on a year to year basis can be a great way to grow. Although I would caution you to not beat yourself up if you didn't grow as much as you think you should have. To me any growth in a positive direction is good.

I often find that as I take time to stop and think about the past year I generally remember things that I had forgotten about. It is in those moments of reflection that I find encouragement and a renewed sense of desire to be better.

Think about things that have changed in your children's lives, grandchildren's lives, in your relationship with a spouse, maybe a relationship with a family member or a friend that was severed but is now healed. Reflect on bills that were paid that required you to trust in Jesus for, and miraculously the money came in, situations that you were so worried and concerned about and now as you reflect, you can see God's hand was on them the whole time.

I never want to become stagnant in my relationship with the Lord or in my life in general. Think about things that sit stagnant, they are smelly, moldy and disgusting. I never want to be smelly and moldy! When we are moving, and growing things will never get to that stagnant place.

By encouraging yourself to be better and stronger, it makes room for opportunity for the Lord to be more effective through you. As I make a conscious effort to do that each and every year, I truly see changes in my life. It isn't an unattainable goal like a resolution, because I know it will take the year to accomplish. I can't stop in a month and reflect on how well I did. I need the year to have a substantial amount of time to reflect upon.

Giving myself the year also makes room for mistakes and learning. We are not always going to get things right. Sometimes we go off on our own little tangents and we will need to stop, pick ourselves up again, dust off, and get started again. The beauty of reflecting each New Year is we get to see where we failed, but also how we persevered and made it better afterwards.

I will never say I have arrived! We are always learning and changing. My goal is to learn and change for the positive; to be more and more Christ-like each and every day. Even Paul states in Philippians 3:13 that he strains forward continually towards the goals that the Lord has set out for him. He knew the importance of constantly moving forward and not focusing on the past. (We will discuss "past stuff" on Day 16) Maybe it's not the New Year for you as you read this devotional, but you don't need to wait until New Years Eve to make that commitment to move forward for Him. Make today the day you choose to be better than you were yesterday and even today!

Prayer For Today:

Lord, I must admit there have been moments that I have decided to remain in my comfort zone out of fear or uncertainty. I pray that you will help me to reflect honestly on my life. I want to be better all the time for you. I want to see positive changes in my life on an ongoing basis. I don't want to become stagnant and smelly. But I want to have the aroma of Christ in my life. That all who see me would see you and not me.
Amen.

DAY 15 | Challenge

Today's Date: _____

1. Take some time to think about what makes you happy. What would your perfect me-time look like? Write that down here.
2. Look at your day and figure out at what point in the day you could carve out enough time to have some me-time.
3. Set yourself a reminder on your phone or your day timer that you have a "daily appointment" with yourself for some much needed me-time!
4. Find an accountability partner who will check on you once in awhile to make sure you are sticking to your guilt-free me-time.
5. Have your accountability partner read this part of your journal and sign on the bottom of this page that they will keep you accountable.

_____
_____
_____
_____
_____

Things I Learned About Myself Today.

Today's Date: _____

_____

_____

_____

_____

_____

_____

_____

_____

_____

_____

_____

_____

_____

_____

_____

_____

_____

_____

_____

_____

DAY 16

It's A New Day

It's A New Day

Truth To Stand On:

Therefore, if anyone is in Christ, the new creation has come: The old has gone, the new is here! All this is from God, who reconciled us to Himself through Christ and gave us the ministry of reconciliation.
–2 Corinthians 5-17-18 (NIV)

I am currently the lead pastor of a church that is referred to as a "Re-Plant". My husband Darrel, my daughter Tamara and I came here to restart this church. It had been closed for just over 2 years prior to our arrival. God has certainly done amazing things here since we have reopened the church doors and we have seen His hand on us and this ministry all along the way.

The road to opening the church was not always an easy one, I have to admit. But we remained believing that this was God's will and we persevered. We often received negative comments from people who have been around the area and thought it was a huge mistake to try to re-open this church. My husband and I decided that the only way we could shut down the naysayers was to quickly come back with what became our famous tagline, "It's a New Day"!

So often we have those naysayers in our lives that try to over-shadow us with their negative opinions. As I sit and reflect on all that God has done here in this community since this church has reopened I find myself overwhelmed and in awe of God's power and His faithfulness and grace. Imagine if we would have given an ear to those who thought it was such a horrible idea to re-open the church. I think about the lives that have been changed over these past few years; all the ones who have come to have a relationship with Christ, the marriages that have been healed, lives that now have hope again, and families that are growing up with the Lord in the centre of their home. All this would not have happened had we listened to those pessimistic voices and decided that they were correct.

In the beginning weeks and months after re-opening, we would sit at the window of the church on a Sunday morning hoping and waiting to see if anyone would show up to our service. In those challenging moments watching the clock, the comments from the negative people would come back into our minds. There were many, many weeks that we would have 1 or 2 people come to church. I laugh now as I think about it, those poor people sitting in the pews as I preached to them as if there were 300 present that day. Doing announcements, preaching, worship, everything as if the church was full.

We truly believed God had called us there. We had to completely rely on Him and what we knew to be His truth. And so, we persevered each and every week trusting that God would fill that place once again. Now two and half years later we are seeking ways to put more seats in our building. God came through and did indeed fill this place! All for His glory! Sometimes we need to be reminded that there will always be negative nellies out there. The world is full of them; people who simply choose to not see the good or potential in anything, the ones who know your past, knew you before and seem to have an idea that you will never change, the ones who can't see beyond what once was. But we have God in us! He sees the potential and the good that can come when we surrender everything to Him. He doesn't dwell on what was past, He sees what can be! He sees the New Day! The New you! We need to sit back and say, "OK Lord, have your way in us!!!" And agree with Him that YES, it is a NEW DAY!

In Philippians 3:13-14 the writer, Paul talks about this very thing. He was a guy who had a very horrible past. He was a leader who hunted down anyone who called themselves a follower of Christ. He would have them either killed or put in jail. Saul (his former name before he became Paul) was a man that was hated and feared by multitudes of people. God, in His amazing unconditional love, sought out Saul on the road to Damascus. Saul ended up having an amazing experience with Christ and fully gave his life over to Him. He turned his life completely around and became the most amazing missionary for the gospel!

In this scripture Paul talks about forgetting the past, and straining forward towards the future. He decided to put what was past to an end and move forward onto all that God had for him! He was basically saying, "It's a new day!" I am sure there were many people who would have tried to bring him down. Just like how we have the disapproving critics in this day and age, they were certainly present in Paul's day as well. People who feel the need to let us, and everyone else know that they do not see any way that any good can come from us or our efforts.

Just as Paul made the decision to put the past away, so we need to do the same. As you are reading this book and doing the challenges you are becoming a new person! It's a new day for you! You are not who you were. You are becoming stronger every day. Any time you feel that negative voice trying to speak into your life, go to the scripture and read this verse! With Christ on your side you will never go wrong! You too will have as incredible of a testimony as we do in regards to this church. A testimony that speaks of the glory of God and a life changed because of Him.

Prayer For Today:

Dear Lord, thank you that past is past! You choose to remember it no more. Thank you that I am a new creation. Thank you that it is a new day! Even when I make mistakes you will still love me no matter what. You are the God of second, third and fourth chances! Help me Lord, to be like Paul, and keep my focus on the future and all the incredible things that we will accomplish together. I strain forward towards the goal you have for me! I give you praise and glory for what is to come. And I choose to not allow the negative voices to speak into my life any longer!
Amen.

DAY 16 | Challenge

Today's Date: _____

1. Write yourself a letter, reminding yourself that you are a new creation and today is a new day!
2. On a separate piece of paper write down who you were in the past. Then rip it up into pieces and throw it in the garbage as a declaration that you are no longer that person!
3. Come back and list on this paper who you are now and who you want to be in the future!

_____

_____

_____

_____

_____

_____

Things I Learned About Myself Today.

Today's Date: _____

_____

_____

_____

_____

_____

_____

_____

_____

_____

_____

_____

_____

_____

_____

_____

_____

_____

_____

_____

_____

DAY 17

Happiness Versus Joy

Happiness Versus Joy

Truth To Stand On:

As the Father has loved me, so I have loved you. Now remain in my love. If you keep my commands, you will remain in my love, just as I have kept my Father's commands and remain in his love. I have told you this so that my joy may be in you and that your joy may be complete.
–John 15:9-11 (NIV)

Whenever I think of the word happy, I hear the voice of Phil Robertson from Duck Dynasty; "Happy, Happy, Happy!"

So many of us base our lives on the emotion of being happy. If life, or our spouse, or our children, or our jobs don't make us happy we are not too pleasant to be around. Oftentimes, we seek out happiness to bring what we think is completion to our lives and we are left disappointed. Many times, during my years of ministry I have heard people lamenting that their spouse just doesn't make them "happy" anymore. And from that, often a decision is made to leave the relationship.

We can put so much pressure on outside sources to bring us happiness. The problem with that way of thinking is that the ones we are putting this pressure on are human and come with faults. I often remind my congregation from the pulpit of my humanness, and that I will irritate them at some point if I haven't already. None of us are perfect. Surprise! The only one who is perfect, and is the only one who really matters, is Christ!

Interestingly enough, God does not promise us happiness in scripture anywhere! This may come as a shock to you, but God is not really interested in your happiness! I am sure there are a few of you who need to pick yourself up off the floor right now! HAHAHA! (You can Google it if you don't believe me. But you won't find anywhere that God wants you to be happy.)

Happiness is an emotion and is triggered by external sources. Since it is triggered by outside sources it is also removed by outside sources as well. A great way to understand this is to picture a little happy face emoji laying on your chest. Anything can touch it and destroy it. Rain, wind, a person's hand can come along and rip it up into a million pieces. And you are left with nothing. It is a huge target ready and waiting to be destroyed.

When we rely on others for happiness we will be disappointed at some point, that I can assure you.

God wants us to find joy. Now that is something He promises in scripture! The difference with joy is that it is triggered from internal sources. So that means that it is inside of you. It is protected from all storms and winds that may come.

In John 15:9-12 we are taught that Christ gives us joy as we remain in Him. As long as we maintain a relationship with Christ and focus on Him we will have joy. It doesn't mean that we will never have problems ever again. But it does mean that He will be with us in every situation, and He will not leave us or forsake us. As long as we lean on Him He will give us the peace and joy that we need to continue on in life.

When we struggle with insecurities we tend to look to people to make us feel better about ourselves, rather than looking to Christ. When we do that we receive a temporary fix to our problem. No matter how incredible our spouse, our friends or family, they are not perfect. God is. In Him we find perfect joy. He is the only one who can bring that peace and assurance into your life.

Allow me to encourage you today to dig even deeper into your relationship with Him. I am often asked why I am so happy all the time. I can honestly say it is truly because I remain in Christ daily! I have had my share of troubled times. There are moments that I think back to all the bumps and mountains that my husband and I have had to overcome together, as a family, or the ones I had to conquer on my own and I am truly in awe that I am still standing. Life is never easy but I know beyond any shadow of a doubt that God goes with me in all areas of this life, and He will go the journey with me and bring me through stronger than I was before I went in. My joy truly is from Him! And there is nothing external that can ever take that away from me.

Choose today the joy that comes from Christ! I promise, you will not be disappointed!

Prayer For Today:

Lord, today I make the choice to remain in your love and keep your commands. Forgive me for the times I have looked to people to bring me happiness. I know that you are the only one who can bring true joy to my life. I thank you for that joy because it cannot be taken away from me. Thank you for the knowledge that even if the world disappoints me, you never will!! I stand before you now, confident in all that you have for me, that you go with me through every storm and I need not fear anything because you are with me. Amen.

DAY 17 | Challenge

Today's Date: _____

1.   Write a promise to yourself that you will no longer rely on people to make you happy.
2.   Write a declaration to yourself that you choose to rely on Christ for your JOY!
3.   Write out today's "Truth To Stand On" and highlight the word JOY!

_____

_____

_____

_____

_____

_____

_____

Things I Learned About Myself Today.

Today's Date: _____

_____

_____

_____

_____

_____

_____

_____

_____

_____

_____

_____

_____

_____

_____

_____

_____

_____

_____

DAY 18

Who Are YOU

Who Are YOU

Truth To Stand On:

You alone created my inner being. You knit me together inside my mother. I will give thanks to you because I have been so amazingly and miraculously made. Your works are miraculous, and my soul is fully aware of this.
–Psalms 139:13-14 (NIV)

Long before I went to Bible College, and long before I went into ministry, I was first a hairstylist, and well, I still am! HAHA! Doing hair has been an amazing way to not only make a bit of extra money on the side, but it has been a wonderful avenue to do ministry as well. I have been able to take my scissors on mission's trips and quite literally stand on the street and just start doing random peoples hair! Sounds funny but, it works! Who doesn't need a haircut, right? HAHAHA! I have been able to cut hair in a church where I ministered, and do it for free once a month, to anyone who just couldn't afford to get their hair cut. It has just been a great way for people to open up to me in the salon about their personal lives and I have been able to speak God's love to them. God has opened countless doors for ministry through my hairstyling career.

Throughout my 30 + years of doing hair I have had many strange requests from people. Anything from interesting hair colors to clipping names, numbers and odd designs into the hair. I have had people bring in pictures of themselves from 35 years prior and ask me to make them look like that again. I have had people bring in photos of famous people with the face cut out and their face glued in place of the original person! HAHAHA! One dear lady who has passed on now, would draw on new eye brows about 1 inch above her existing eyebrows because she did not like the placement of the real ones. And so, opting for 2 eye brows in her mind was better than one set that were set too low...

We can all laugh at these stories and think these people are, well… let's say interesting… to be kind. But truly aren't we all the same? We all try to change what God gave us in the first place. I will get people with curly hair asking for it to be straightened and people with straight hair ask me to make their hair curly. Thin haired people asking for extensions to make their hair thicker, and thick haired people asking me to take my thinning shears and make it thinner.

I truly think the most interesting question ever asked of me as a stylist has been, "If you were me and you had my hair, what would you do?" Now this is a very difficult question to ask your stylist. For those of you who have ever posed this question to your stylist, here is why it is challenging. As I write this book I have bleach blonde highlights in my hair and one side of my head is shaved to the skin. The other side is angle cut and is long past my chin with long bangs. 6 months ago, I had a completely different style and I can pretty much guarantee in another 6 months from now I will have a completely different style and color yet again. This is because that is who I am. My personality is one that gets bored easily of my hair, and therefore I change it regularly. I am not afraid to try new things, and I like styles that would seem strange or too daring to most.

So when I have a client who has hair down to their waist and it is natural that has never been colored and they ask me what I would do with their hair if it was mine, my answer very likely would be Hmmmmm, I would cut it, shave it, color it, and so on, because that is my personality. After the shock wears off, the client would most likely reply, "OK how about just a trim today?!" HAHAHA!

My point in all this is simply to say we are all different. We all have different likes and dislikes. What works for one may not work for another and that is ok!! That is what makes the world an interesting place. So, let's embrace who we are. To be completely honest when I do get asked that question I begin to answer by asking the person about their personality. What do they like to do with their hair, do they like to take the time to style it? Do they like to keep it long? etc.

It is in the discovering of one's personality that I am then able to find them their perfect hair style. And very likely it will be nothing like what I would do, "if I had their hair!" We often look at other people and are intrigued or fascinated by them and we want to somehow be like them. But it isn't a comfortable place for us because it's not who we really are. So, everyone let me ask you, "Who are you?" Once you figure that out you can be proud of that person and walk boldly in that knowledge! Be comfortable in your personality. There is nothing wrong with who you are! God knit you together in your mother's womb to be who you are today! Embrace that person and be true to who you are!

DAY 18 | Challenge

Today's Date: _____

1. Write out a statement of who you are. What is your personality? Are you bold, are you quiet, loud, adventurous, shy, a homebody? What is your unique personality?
2. .Write out the positives about your personality. How are you able to affect the world for Jesus because of who you are?
3. Copy today's "Truth to Stand On" in your own words thanking God and acknowledging that He created you the way He wanted you to be.

_____

_____

_____

_____

_____

_____

Things I Learned About Myself Today.

Today's Date: _____

_____

_____

_____

_____

_____

_____

_____

_____

_____

_____

_____

_____

_____

_____

_____

_____

_____

_____

_____

_____

DAY 19

God Has Purpose For You!

God Has Purpose For You!

Truth To Stand On:

Yet you, Lord, are our Father. We are the clay, you are the potter; we are all the work of your hand.
–Isaiah 64:8 (NIV)

Yesterday we talked about personalities and how we all have different and unique personalities that were created by our Heavenly Father. Today I would like to continue on that topic and share with you how God can use all types of personalities.

Prior to being a lead pastor of a church, I was a youth pastor for many, many years. I often joke that I was doing youth ministry back when the dinosaurs were around. I have been so blessed to see many teens go forward in their pursuit of Jesus and even some become pastors themselves, which is quite exciting, but at the same time can make me feel a bit old at times! HAHAHA!

In case you haven't picked up on this already, my personality can be pretty out there! I have had the tendency to be a little bit too loud on occasion. My husband has given me the eye from time to time to try to get me to calm down a bit. HAHAHA! (Very brave of him I might add!)
I am not making excuses for how I am, I truly have come to the realization that this is who I am and God has chosen to use this energy I have and excitement for life for His glory! Thank goodness.

During my time leading youth, I had a number of students that came through my ministry who were exact opposite of who I am. And to be honest, I am sure that when they first met me I very likely scared the life out of them! Again, I must thank God for His faithfulness and patience with me in all of this!

It didn't take me long to realize that if I wanted to effectively minister to these students on a level that they would understand and feel comfortable, I needed to pull in some reinforcements. And so, I prayed for God to lead me in what direction I was to go in all of this.

He began to show me different people in my church that had different personalities then I had; personalities that were very similar to some of the students who were coming in on a Friday night. God gave me, what I like to call, my lightbulb moment! These people needed to become youth leaders! And so, the pursuit began.
I would begin the journey of finding leaders who could relate to all different personalities in my group. On many occasions when I would approach people about the idea of helping out in youth ministry, their first response was, "But I'm not like you, all crazy and stuff!!" And my reply every time was "I KNOW! That's exactly why I NEED you!"

You see, some of the students were a bit afraid of me and not so willing to open up to me because I may have well... freaked them out a bit! But having leaders who they could relate to made this ministry so much more powerful. They found in these youth leaders, persons who they could not only relate to, but open up to about personal issues. They were able to do this without fear or feeling uncomfortable. And the best part was that these young people grew in confidence in who they were because they could see it wasn't bad to be quiet or reserved!

I made it my mission to have all kinds of different personality types on my leadership team. God was able to move so powerfully in each group I had the blessing to lead.

Too many times we get in our minds that God can only use the people who are bold and not afraid to get up in front of a crowd. That is such a lie from the enemy! God uses all of us, that is why He created us so differently. We all have different personalities for different purposes.

My husband is the biggest behind-the-scenes guy ever. He loves to fix things, build things, and work in the sound room. The moment you put him in front of a crowd, he shuts down. God uses him behind the scenes so powerfully, it is unreal.

The people and churches that have been blessed by him is amazing.

Allow God to use you and your unique personality for His glory!! You will be shocked at how many lives you will impact because of who you are!

Prayer For Today:

Lord, thank you for being the potter and having me as the clay. I just need to surrender my life to you and you will come in and form me however you need me to be for your glory! This is truly amazing! Thank you for your specific purpose for me. I am thankful that you need my unique personality to be effective for your kingdom! Lord, give me many opportunities to be used by you. Open up doors that I never, ever thought possible!
Amen.

DAY 19 | Challenge

Today's Date: _____

1. Write out ways that you are allowing God to use you right now?
2. Is there any fear within you that is hindering God's plan of using you for His glory? If yes, describe those fears.
3. Ask the Lord to remove the fears and build confidence in you so that you can fulfill His purpose for you!
4. Write a short letter to God telling him that you are going to allow him to form you like the potter forms the clay.

_____

_____

_____

_____

_____

_____

Things I Learned About Myself Today.

Today's Date: _____

_____

_____

_____

_____

_____

_____

_____

_____

_____

_____

_____

_____

_____

_____

_____

_____

_____

_____

_____

DAY 20

It's a Great Day
If You Are Above Ground

It's A Great Day
If You Are Above Ground

Truth To Stand On:

Yet you, Lord, are our Father. We are the clay, you are the potter; we are all the work of your hand.
–Isaiah 64:8 (NIV)

Have you ever heard the saying, "Misery loves company"? Oh, how true that saying is, right? Negative, sad people love to have company in the wallow or pity party. It is somehow oddly comforting I guess to have a person to sit beside you and agree that life is horrible, and we may as well just give up!

When we struggle in a big way with insecurities it doesn't take much to take us down even lower. This is why it is imperative that we surround ourselves with positive people. We slowly become like the people we hang out with the most. Do you ever notice how we pick up words, sayings, and mannerisms from our friends or spouse? I chuckle to myself often when I see myself doing things I know my friends do. For instance, I have a friend who is very Italian! I Love her to pieces! And she talks with her hands all the time. And many times, it's that hand movement that makes the conversation! We all know someone who waves their hands in the air to intensify what they are trying to express. Oftentimes we see Italian people bring their fingers to their mouths to kiss when the food is going to be extremely tasty. You know what I mean. Well, let me just say as I hang out with my sweet Italian friend I find myself copying her with my hand motions! Excuse me! I am German and Dutch! Not Italian! HAHAHA! But this is what happens; we slowly pick up the actions of those around us. So, my friends, be sure to surround yourself with positive people! They are contagious!

Today I had a client in my salon who made me laugh so hard. She told me that she was at work and someone asked her how she was. You know that typical question that no one really wants to know exactly how you are, it's just something we do to try to open up conversation. Well her reply nearly took the man onto the floor with laughter, as it did with me. And here is her reply to her co-worker's question: "Well, I am breathing, standing, above ground, I can pee on my own, eat on my own, and dress myself, so I think it is a great day!" WOW! I love, love, love it! Now that is positive thinking! These are the people we need to surround ourselves with. People who find good in the little things in life.

This world has so much negativity. Watching the news alone can put a person into depression. But we serve a God that is greater than everything and watches over us and cares for us and will never leave us alone. So, we don't need to be afraid or worried about anything.

Sometimes we need to take time to reassess who we spend the majority of our time with, and what kind of influence they have on us.   Life is way too short to spend it with negative people pouring their negative thoughts on us. Now I'm not saying ditch every person who has a bad day, of course. And yes, we need to be Jesus with skin on to everyone. Meaning we need to take time to pour positivity into everyone and try to encourage one another absolutely!! But if it is a situation where that the person is only pulling you down and isn't willing to listen to positive, it is maybe time to cut the ties. Personally, I am able to tear myself down enough on my own without the voice of other people helping me. That is why I find it an absolute necessity to spend time at Jesus' feet daily. I am not strong enough to face a negative world on my own. I need His influence in my ears. I need His voice to be the strongest in my head.

As you spend time with the Lord and allow Him to be the main influence in your life, and top that off by surrounding yourself with people who do the same, you will grow stronger and stronger each and every day.

Prayer For Today:

Lord, thank you for being that positive voice in my ears at all times. Thank you for always being there showing me that you go with me no matter how good or bad life is. I pray that you will help me to stay positive about myself and the world around me. Show me areas in my life I need to change. Show me people in my life that I may need to remove. And show me the ones that I need to surround myself with. Lord, continue to guide me each and every day, so that I can be a positive influence on others around me.
Amen.

DAY 20 | Challenge

Today's Date: _____

1. Take time in prayer asking the Lord if there are people in your life that you need to step away from because of their negative influence.
2. Take time to assess how much time you spend in the presence of the Lord. How much communication do you have with Him and what is His influence on you.
3. Record here what the Lord is saying to you in both these scenarios.

_____

_____

_____

_____

_____

_____

_____

Things I Learned About Myself Today.

Today's Date: _____

_____

_____

_____

_____

_____

_____

_____

_____

_____

_____

_____

_____

_____

_____

_____

_____

_____

_____

_____

DAY 21

Famous Failures

Famous Failures

Truth To Stand On:

For God so loved the world that He gave His only begotten son, that whoever believes in Him will not perish but have eternal life.
–John 3:16 (NIV)

There is a story of Thomas Edison and his mother that I stumbled across a few months ago. I researched what I had read to be sure this story was actually true. Even though there was in fact a small bit of embellishment in the story where I originally read it, it remains a story of great failure but also great success.

As Thomas was in school as a child he struggled deeply with learning. One day during school hours he overheard his teacher talking to the principal of the school. The teacher informed the principal that Thomas was "addled" (which meant he was not very smart). The teacher proceeded to say it would not be worthwhile to keep him in school. Thomas went home devastated, and in tears, crying to his mother telling her what he had overheard. His mother went into, what I like to call, "mother bear mode". She marched into the school and gave the teacher and principal a strong worded speech. Letting them know quite frankly that they were, in fact, the ones with the learning problem and that she will take him out of school and teach him at home herself.

At 16 years of age after being taught by his courageous and cheerleader of a mom, Thomas ventured out on his own. At 22 years of age he invented the 1st electrographic vote-recorder, which enabled legislators in the U.S. congress to record votes in a more efficient manner than the voice voting system that had been used for years. He proceeded to invent many other important items that have quite literally changed the world; the light bulb, motion picture and phonograph, to name a few.

He is an incredible story of someone who was considered to be a failure that turned into someone who became an incredible history maker! In a very rare interview he gave all the credit of his grand success to his mother. He stated, "she believed in me when no one else would!" When I read those words, I couldn't help but think of Jesus! He believes in us when no one else will.

Jesus is our biggest cheerleader! He sees the potential in us above what everyone else sees in us. He knew that in and of ourselves, we are failures, that we sin, and we fall short on a daily basis, But He still believes in us. He believes in us so strongly that He was willing to go to the cross and die for us so that we could have eternity with Him. And the best part for each and every one of us to know is that He would have done this for us even if we were the only person on this earth. It is sometimes difficult for us to comprehend this depth of love. But that is exactly what Christ did for us. He took all our sins, our shortcomings, our "addled" moments, and took them to the cross as a final blood sacrifice for the forgiveness of our sin and mistakes. He didn't want us to have to settle for a life without greatness, and peace, and grace. He wanted the absolute best for us, just like Thomas's mother wanted for him.

Thomas allowed his mom to teach him daily and pour all that she knew into him. And from that gift that she gave him he became one of the greatest successes the world has ever known. Jesus wants to do the same for you and for me. All we have to do is allow Him to do so. He is standing at your door knocking. Will you let Him in? Will you allow Jesus to pour himself into you to help teach you, guide you, and lead you, so that you too can become the best version of YOU ever!

The world will try to tell you that you are unfit. But Christ is telling you different! He is telling you that He loves you unconditionally and wants the absolute best for you. If you have never made a decision to follow Christ, to surrender your life completely to Him so that He can be that voice of truth in your ears, can I encourage you today to make that decision? This will be the best decision you have ever made in your life that I can promise you without a question in my mind.

DAY 21 | Challenge

Today's Date: _____

1. If you have never made the decision to follow Christ before, I encourage you to do so today.
2. If you have made this commitment before, but have fallen away, I challenge you to recommit to Him today.

   Make notes about your decision to remember this day and your choice to follow Christ.

   If you made a decision to follow Christ today. Find a friend who is a follower of Christ and tell them. Ask them to help you begin this new journey. If you don't know anyone please contact me via my website: www.contagiouspower.ca and I will do my best to give you some guidance.

_____

_____

_____

Things I Learned About Myself Today.

Today's Date: _____

_____

_____

_____

_____

_____

_____

_____

_____

_____

_____

_____

_____

_____

_____

_____

_____

_____

_____

_____

DAY 22

"We Buy Ugly Houses"

"We Buy Ugly Houses"

Truth To Stand On:

He leads me beside still waters and He refreshes my soul.
–Psalms 23:2-3 (NIV)

A few years ago, I saw a huge billboard sign that stated very boldly… "We Buy Ugly Houses". I honestly cannot remember where I was when I saw this sign. My life brings me to so many different locations that I don't recall if it was in Canada or the USA that I saw this sign. But I do remember the laughter that came from my mouth as I drove by the sign. At first as I read it, I thought I was seeing things. But sure enough, as I drove closer to the billboard it actually did say what I had thought I read.

How crazy it seemed that a company would seek out "ugly" houses. And who would want to admit that their house was ugly anyway. I assume that this company would purchase homes for a low price and then fix them up to be something spectacular afterwards. And again, I think it would be safe to assume that the old, ugly house's new value would be substantially higher than the "ugly house" value. All this old, ugly home needed was someone to come along and give it some time and effort to help it to be something incredible.

When we hear the words "Ugly Houses", if you are like me, I would automatically assume that these homes are really not worth putting the time and effort into. Sometimes it's hard to imagine something so bad being turned into anything good. I think of my husband who needs visuals when we go clothes shopping for him. He likes to do what we have now called, "mannequin shopping". When I try to get him to make a purchase, he says he needs to see it on a mannequin first to know what it will actually look like. For him to imagine in his mind how things will look on him is next to impossible. So, we search out mannequins to help this shopping process along.

But this company looks at these "ugly houses" in a whole new way. They have the ability to look at something that is run down and in disrepair and see it for what it can be; without the mannequin. While many of us would discount these homes and think there is no hope for them, they see them as a gold mine. They see beyond the surface and look much, much deeper. They see the potential of what can be if given a chance.

Imagine the before and after pictures of these homes. People would be astounded, I am sure. "Is this really the same home? Impossible!" I can almost guarantee that this business would grow exponentially simply from word of mouth. After people see the transformations of these houses, they won't be able to stop talking about this company and all it has to offer.

This is so much like what Christ does for us! We may see ourselves as an "Ugly House", old, run down, and in disrepair. But Christ sees us as a gold mine. We see all the work and expense it will take to make us new again and appealing to others. But He sees us as something that is certainly worth every minute it will take to make us better.

And the best part is, He doesn't only want to help repair all the damage and hurt that we have in our homes, but He wants to live with us there as well. He sees all the broken windows, the cracked ceilings, the unlevel flooring and none of it scares Him away. He knows that deep down inside is something incredible waiting to come out. And He longs to find a home in there not just a house.

He sees substantial worth in us! He is seeking us out in earnest to help us become a beautiful and restored home for His glory. As others see the changes in us, inside and out, they will be drawn to Christ as well. We will become walking billboards for Jesus!

Yesterday I gave you a challenge to allow Christ to come into your life; to allow Him to lead and guide you. As you go forward in your relationship with Him He will continue to make your house a beautiful home! What others may have seen as worthless and ugly He sees as one that is simply in need of a bit of repair with much love, care, and grace.

Prayer For Today:

Dear Lord, thank you for still working in the repair business. Thank you for your willingness to take the time to help build me back up again and renew me. Thank you for looking at me with love and grace and seeing all that I can be in you. Lord, I want to be a home for you to live in. I give you permission to move in my life how you see the need.
Amen.

DAY 22 | Challenge

Today's Date: _____

1. With all repairs and renovations on a home comes a lot of garbage that needs to be thrown away. Write here all the things in your life that are garbage and need to be thrown out for good.
2. Picture yourself actually taking these things to the trash. Leaving them on the side of the road for the garbage truck to pick up and take away forever!
3. Make a promise here to yourself, that you will not go to the dump site and pick those things up again.

_____

_____

_____

_____

_____

_____

Things I Learned About Myself Today.

Today's Date: _____

_____

_____

_____

_____

_____

_____

_____

_____

_____

_____

_____

_____

_____

_____

_____

_____

_____

_____

DAY 23

Proverbs 31 Woman

Proverbs 31 Woman

Truth To Stand On:

"She is clothed with dignity and strength"
–Proverbs 31:25 (NIV)

The other day I was in a mall with one of my daughters. We were walking by a lingerie store and I almost fell over in shock as I took a glance at the posters in the window. Now I know what you are thinking, "Yes Wendy, it is a lingerie store. What are you expecting?". But no, you don't even understand! What I saw was pictures of models with stretch marks on their legs and areas of cellulite! YES CELLULITE! I could not believe my eyes! I actually wanted to take a picture of the poster and share my findings on social media! But my daughter very strongly let me know that would not be appropriate! HAHAHA! But I was in such shock! And to be completely honest, I must admit, I was a little bit happy too! You mean, they are REAL LIVE WOMEN with CELLULITE?! Sorry! As you can see I am still not completely over the shock.

My daughter, the wise young woman that she is, informed me that yes, in fact modelling agencies are trying to promote "normal-looking" women and not do as much air brushing and editing that they normally do. Well alleluia it's about time someone figured this out! HAHA! So much emphasis is put on our outward appearance that the news about modelling agencies changing their perspective is incredible.

There is a story of a woman in the bible that is referred to as "The Wife of Noble Character", or many of us will know her as the Proverbs 31 Woman.

The interesting thing that I love about the description of this woman is that never once do we hear anything about her physical appearance. She is famous, known by many. Yet her fame does not come from outward beauty.

In our world today much depends on our outward appearance. Statistics will tell us that when applying for a job, many times outward appearance will have an effect on whether we receive the job or not. I recently saw a video of a test that was done with a child who was dressed in clean, expensive clothes going into a restaurant, crying, looking for her mom that she had somehow been separated from. All the people were drawn to her and did all that they could do to reunite mother and child. And then they took the same child and put her in dirty clothes, and made her face dirty and did the same test in another restaurant. The child was ignored and shooed away. It is physical appearances that many times make the decision for us as to whether that person is worth our time or not.

But here in the Proverbs 31 Woman's story she is held in the highest regard for her character, not for her appearance.

This scripture tells us she is more precious than rubies. She gets up in the morning to care for her family and make them breakfast, to be sure they start their day with a healthy meal. She has integrity and does all business in an upright and honorable way. When she speaks, she speaks with wisdom and doesn't gossip or speak negatively of others. She is a hard worker, taking care in all her daily chores. Her husband can trust her and doesn't have to worry that she is flirting with others. She helps the poor and lives life with no fear. She is a woman of dignity and honor.

This is how I want to be known. I don't want to be only known for my physical features, but I want to be known as a woman of dignity and honor; a woman that is real and not touched-up by modern technology.

Proverbs 31: 30 tells us "Charm is deceptive, and beauty does not last; but a woman who fears the Lord will be greatly praised."

This is who I want to be! How about you?

DAY 23 | Challenge

Today's Date: _____

1. Write out Proverbs 31:10-31
2. Write out any changes that God may be speaking to you about in regard to your inward character.
3. Write a commitment to the Lord on how you will make those changes. Be specific.
4. Find a close friend who you can share those changes with and ask them to keep you accountable.

_____

_____

_____

Things I Learned About Myself Today.

Today's Date: _____

_____

_____

_____

_____

_____

_____

_____

_____

_____

_____

_____

_____

_____

_____

_____

_____

_____

_____

DAY 24

Power Of Our Words!

Power Of Our Words!

Truth To Stand On:

Gentle words bring life and health: a deceitful tongue crushes the spirit
–Proverbs 15:4 (NIV)

Have you ever stopped to consider the power of our words? Think about all the negative things that have been spoken over you in your lifetime. And now think about the amount of time it has, or is taking to get over those words. Words have so much power in them.

I remember as kid coming home from school and being so upset because of words that were spoken about me, and to me by kids on the playground. My mother would repeatedly say to me, "Honey, just remember sticks and stones can break your bones, but words can never hurt you!" When I think about that little saying now I have come to the conclusion that it is one big fat lie! Sure, those words may not hurt me physically, like a broken bone, but emotionally the damage can be as painful if not more so. Words have great power to them.

Think about the story of creation in the book of Genesis in the bible. Genesis 1:3. We see God speaking the world into existence. God said: "Let there be light", and it was so!

Vs 6 God said, "Let there be a vault between the waters to separate water from water" and it was so!

Vs 11 God said, "Let the land produce vegetation" and it was so!

On and on we see words spoken and then followed by "it was so".

There is great power in words. God tells us in the New Testament that we will have His power in us when we follow Him.

So that means our words have power as well. What we speak into the atmosphere will "be so"! We need to be cautious with what we speak out. We need to watch what we speak about ourselves, but as well, we need to watch what we speak aloud about others. We have the ability to speak life and death over people and ourselves.

We can see this with all the people who struggle with insecurities. It all mostly stems from words spoken over us that were in a negative context. We hear these words and we begin to believe what they are saying to us. We often bring to life those hurtful words that were said to us.

The story of Gideon in the book of Judges is an incredible story. I love this story because Gideon is called out by God to do the miraculous. We first find Gideon in this story hiding from the enemy in a wine press. God gives a message to an angel to share with Gideon. He calls Gideon a Mighty Warrior! Here we see Gideon hiding. I translate Gideon's response to the angel as, "Um, excuse me, but who are you calling mighty warrior? Don't you know I am the least of my clan and not only am I the least of my clan, but my clan is the least of all the clans combined." Talk about some serious insecurities!

But God looked at Gideon as the man He knew he could become! God was speaking Life over Gideon! He was speaking words of growth and ability and strength over him! As we continue to read the story we see Gideon indeed became that Mighty Warrior!

Power in our words. Let's speak life into our own lives! Let's speak life into the people around us. Let's speak life into our spouse's lives. Let's speak life into our children! Maybe at this moment they may be the least of the clan but if we speak life into them and believe that God is able then, "It will be so"!

DAY 24 | Challenge

Today's Date: _____

1.   Take whatever negative words that have been spoken over you in the past and write down the opposite of those comments here.
2.   Write out positive words towards people in your life. Spouse, children, sisters, brothers, mother, father, friends, neighbors, etc.

_____

_____

_____

_____

_____

_____

_____

_____

Things I Learned About Myself Today.

Today's Date: _____

_____

_____

_____

_____

_____

_____

_____

_____

_____

_____

_____

_____

_____

_____

_____

_____

_____

_____

_____

DAY 25

The Pink Pen

The Pink Pen

Truth To Stand On:

Gentle words bring life and health: a deceitful tongue crushes the spirit
–Proverbs 15:4 (NIV)

About 6 months ago I was asked to be on the Western Ontario District's Church Planting team for Pentecostal Assemblies of Canada. A huge honour, I might add. This team seeks out people interested in starting new churches around our Ontario district. And we work as not only partners, but mentors with them along this journey. It is truly a very exciting ministry to be a part of. A few weeks ago, we had our first church planting forum. So, attending this meeting were people from all over coming to see what this church planting thing is all about and if they actually want to pursue this next step in their ministry.

As the meeting was about to begin one of leaders proceeded to pass out pens and highlighters to all of us to use for notes in the meeting. This became a "AH-HA" moment for me. Sounds a little strange, I know. How can a pen be an awakening moment?! Well, allow me to explain. All the pens were different colors; blue, orange, red, and pink. When he came to me I stared at the pens like it was a decision of lifetime. "Oh my gosh, what color do I choose!?" Well I am super proud to say I chose PINK!

I am sure by now you are seriously thinking Wendy has lost her mind! It is a Pen! Big deal!" But yes, it is actually a HUGE DEAL! And here is why:

I am a woman lead pastor in a predominantly male world. There are not too many of us women lead pastors out there. I am thrilled to know a few, and we are like a strong team encouraging each other along this journey. Many have called us trailblazers, but I just like to think that I am fulfilling the call of God on my life. But in saying all of that, there are moments where I have felt that I need to somehow hide my femininity. Sounds crazy, I know. I am a woman and am not trying to look like a man but somehow feel like I need to hide the feminine part of me because maybe it will represent weakness.

When I purchased a new bible last year I bought a turquoise blue one rather than the other pastel colors that were offered. My notebook I am currently using is blue and yellow. You see where I am going with this. I know it probably sounds crazy to many of you. But again, don't all our personal insecurities sound crazy to others? How many times have we heard others ask, "Why are you insecure about that?". Who knows why or what goes on in our brains to make us feel inferior. But it is what we do with those feelings, right?!

Now when this wonderful gentleman came by with the opportunity to choose a new Pen or highlighter in a bold new color I had a choice to make. Am I going to revert back to the blue mode again, trying to seem less feminine, or am I going to embrace the fact that yes, I am a woman, and yes, I actually like pink! So, I am the proud new owner of a very bright PINK pen. And guess what? The world did not come crashing down. No one looked at me like, "Oh my goodness, she is not only a female pastor, but she has a pink pen too! How can she ever lead a church properly?!" HAHAHA! None of that happened. This was a defining moment for me, as ludicrous as it seems. In my mind I took a stand and affirmed that, yes, I am free to be who I am, who God created me to be and yes, I am a woman in ministry. Now no one in the room was celebrating with me; in fact, no one else would have even known what was going on in my brain at the time. Well until now, HAHA! But it was a moment of celebration for me internally! And to be honest I look forward to more moments like this because I feel it is making me stronger each and every time.

We need to be proud of who we are and who God has called us to be. No matter if we are male or female. Again, let me reassure you that God created you and me and we are perfectly and wonderfully made! God actually knows what he is doing! Why do we feel we need to hide from that?

DAY 25 | Challenge

Today's Date: _____

1. What areas in your life have made you feel like you are inferior to others around you?
2. How can you change your thinking and embrace those areas?
3. Make a plan to celebrate with someone as you embrace those areas!

_____

_____

_____

_____

_____

_____

_____

_____

Things I Learned About Myself Today.

Today's Date: _____

_____

_____

_____

_____

_____

_____

_____

_____

_____

_____

_____

_____

_____

_____

_____

_____

_____

_____

_____

DAY 26

"Be A Risk-Taker!"

"Be A Risk-Taker!"

Truth To Stand On:

Let us therefore come boldly to the throne of grace, that we may obtain mercy and find grace to help in time of need.
–Hebrews 4:16 (NIV)

Oftentimes we use our insecurities as a crutch. We allow them to stop us from achieving great things in life. Fear sets in and then the mind begins to tell us how we are unable to accomplish the task. Voices in our brain and outside voices only add to the fear.

We need to come to the place in our lives that we use those insecurities as motivators to help us press on to get out of our box and be a risk-taker.

In Luke 18 there is a story of a man who was blind, sitting on the side of the road, begging for enough money to feed himself and to survive. One day as he was going about his normal routine of begging he heard a ruckus around him. And he asked his fellow beggar friends what all that noise was about. They told him it was Jesus and he was coming by. There was a buzz around the area of this man named Jesus who was performing miracles and healing people.

As soon as the blind man heard Jesus getting closer he began to shout out in a very loud voice for Jesus to come to him. Here is a man who had no hope in life, and sat day in and day out on the side of the road stuck in his situation. But today was his moment, his chance to finally break free from this life and have a chance at a better one. As he shouted he heard voices around him telling him to be quiet. His actions were inappropriate for the time. A blind man or anyone inferior should never bother a teacher or leader with his problems. "Leave Jesus alone!" were the words directed at him. But he chose to ignore those replies. He called out even louder "Jesus, have mercy on me!" And it worked. He got Jesus' attention.

Jesus came to him, and after some discussion the man received his sight. He experienced an incredible miracle that would not have happened had he listened to the voices inside of him and around him. He chose to fight against all the odds. He chose to go against normal protocol and step out and ask for healing. He chose to take a risk of being shunned, embarrassed, and possibly disciplined in a harsh manner because he wanted to receive his sight. He pressed on and received the prize.

We need to be risk-takers. Yes, there may be moments where we will fail. But failure is how we learn and grow. Some of those risks will work out to our benefit. Just as our blind friend in this story experienced. If it was not for his risk- taking he would have continued his life begging on the side of the road for his daily meal until the day he died. He was not happy with that scenario. He wanted more. So, he stood up against all odds and pressed on.

On one of my workout D.V.D.'s that I am currently using, the instructor makes an interesting statement that truly keeps me motivated. She says, "It's not always easy, not always fun, but you gotta do it, it's what's gonna get you to your goal!" I have to admit, there are times that I want to jump into that T.V and tell her to be quiet! But she is right. Exercising is not always easy, not always fun, but the truth is, it is getting me to my goal.

Taking a risk is not always easy. But we have got to overcome our insecurities and press on so that we aren't that person sitting on the sidelines watching the world go by and wishing we could have been a part of it!

I am going to end today's devotional with one more quote that is ringing in my mind as I am typing. It is from the infamous Miss Frizzle from the kid's TV show "Magic School Bus"

"Take chances, make mistakes, get messy."

Be encouraged today to yell a little louder, be a little bolder and get the miracle you are looking for!

Prayer For Today:

Lord, I stand before you and shout in a loud voice "I NEED YOU!" Hear my cry oh Lord, and help me to step out of my box and only listen to your voice and no one else's. I don't want to miss out on a thing that you have planned out for me! I know it may not always be easy, but as long as you go with me I know I can't go wrong! Amen!

DAY 26 | Challenge

Today's Date: _____

1. What do you need to shout out to God today? Write it out here.
2. Now write out your declaration of how you will stop listening to the outside voices and step into God's plans for you!

_____

_____

_____

_____

_____

_____

_____

_____

Things I Learned About Myself Today.

Today's Date: _____

_____
_____
_____
_____
_____
_____
_____
_____
_____
_____
_____
_____
_____
_____
_____
_____
_____
_____
_____

DAY 27

Active Plan

Active Plan

Truth To Stand On:

Finally, brothers and sisters, whatever is true, whatever is noble, whatever is right, whatever is pure, whatever is lovely, whatever is admirable – if anything is excellent or praiseworthy – think about such things.
–Philippians 4:8 (NIV)

In the very beginning of this journey I shared with you some issues I had with my physical body. These issues became so debilitating to me that at one point I decided surgery was an EXCELLENT idea. If I could change my body to be the way I thought it should be then at last, my life would be perfect! I talked with my husband and with much begging and pleading on my part, he finally gave in and agreed. But he agreed, only if this was going to finally make me happy and cause me to stop complaining. He stressed that he loved me just the way I was, but he was also growing weary of hearing me go on and on about how horrible my body was. So, I booked an appointment and the journey towards my perceived better life began.

Then it happened; God stepped in. Late one night as I was sitting in my bed thinking about the surgery and how wonderful it was going to be, God began to speak to my heart and mind. The question I heard Him ask me was, "Why do you want to change what I created so perfectly and wonderfully?" I honestly had no answer to give Him. I only had excuses. And then came the next question, "Who are you doing this for?" If my husband and God are happy with the way I looked, why would I need to change that? "Who are you trying to impress?"

This was the most difficult and awkward moment I have ever experienced with God. I had no answers for Him. I suddenly realized I wanted to change my appearance for others because I was bothered by how they looked at me. I then began to think about what I would tell my daughters as they grew up. What would they think? Did God make a mistake? Would I then put ideas in their minds that if they weren't happy with certain parts of their bodies then they too could just go get surgery to have the proper changes made? Is this the impression I wanted to give them? No, not at all! I want them to grow up being proud of who they are and what they look like! But how could I expect that of them if I changed my physical body with surgery. How could I ever tell them that they don't need to if I found it necessary?

I knew then I had to cancel all appointments and begin this journey of finding a way to love myself.

Along my journey I found creative ways to help me feel better about myself. Maybe some of these ideas will help you.

I had a true hatred for me feet. My sister in-law suggested that I go and get a pedicure. Reluctantly, I did. And well, let me tell you, not only was it the best, most relaxing experience ever, I came out feeling like I could show my feet off to the world! They looked AWESOME! I'm a regular now! HAHA!

My hair is so thin, and I hate how it looks scraggly all the time. As much as I would love nothing more than to run my fingers through it and it look all shiny and fall ever so incredibly back into place. (all in slow motion of course like on TV) I have opted for a short, cute, stylish cut. And it looks awesome. Well, in my opinion anyway! HAHAHA! I know at what length it starts to get ratty looking so that is my cue to chop it before the feelings of YUCK begin to invade!

My weight has been a battle forever. I will never be, nor do I want to be, a size 2. Those days are long gone. I choose to be healthy. And I workout and watch what I eat. Will I never have a piece of cake again? Bite your tongue! Of course, I will, but all in moderation. Weight won't come off in a day. It is a long, slow process that takes dedication and determination. All I can say is stick to it! Slow and steady wins the race!

All these things help me to love myself just the way I am, without surgery!

Can I encourage you to find what will help you to feel better about yourself and DO IT!

DAY 27 | Challenge

Today's Date: _____

1.   What is your active plan to begin the journey to loving yourself?

_____

_____

_____

_____

_____

_____

_____

_____

Things I Learned About Myself Today.

Today's Date: _____

_____

_____

_____

_____

_____

_____

_____

_____

_____

_____

_____

_____

_____

_____

_____

_____

_____

_____

_____

_____

DAY 28

Be Strong And Courageous

Be Strong And Courageous

Truth To Stand On:

For God has not given us a spirit of fear; but of power, and of love, and of a sound mind.
–2 Timothy 1:7 (NIV)

The words "Be strong and courageous" were spoken by the Lord in the book of Joshua, chapter 1. Joshua was about to go on a journey of entering the Promised Land. It was now time for him to step up to the plate as leader over the Israelites. And God encouraged him with those powerful words! "BE STRONG AND COURAGEOUS"! And God also reminded Joshua that He will be with him along the journey.

Along the journey of writing this devotional I have shared my innermost feelings and insecurities. I would love to tell you that I have got all my stuff together now and I am perfectly healed of it all, never to question myself ever again! Wouldn't that be amazing? Unfortunately, I can't say that with a complete honest heart. But what I can say is that I am 99.9% better than I was! It has been a journey of years trying to get over words that have been spoken to me and feelings of inability and inadequacy. I truly can say that by the grace of God I am stronger, bolder and much, much more confident.

I have learned to love myself and love who Christ made me to be. I can laugh at myself and not take myself too seriously now. I know beyond a shadow of a doubt the call God has on my life and I will not allow the enemy to try to take that away from me. This is who I am and will be forever!

It is important for us to remember that everyone has some kind of insecurity. We are not alone in this world. I can only hope that as I have shared my stories, that you have somehow been able to find yourself in there somewhere. If this book and my sharing and rawness was simply for you to see that you are not the only one who has ever felt that way, then I would have to say my mission has been accomplished. You are NOT alone! You are not weird, you are not strange. You are 100% normal!

Will you ever be completely over your insecurities? Probably not. Only because each day brings new challenges and new issues that we will have to face. But the question is, how will you face them? Will you cower and go it alone and give up? Or will you stand in faith believing that God goes with you and He is standing beside you, cheering you on loudly and exuberantly; "BE STRONG AND COURAGEOUS!" "I AM WITH YOU!"

Many of us have gone to the altar at church and begged God to take away these insecurities. Many of us have sat in our bedrooms and prayed that exact prayer. Only to go back to normal life and find the insecurities are still there. And then we get mad at God because He didn't take them away. Here is what we need to remember; we are a team with the Lord as our captain. He doesn't wave a magic wand and, *poof*, we are perfect and feel wonderful about ourselves and go on our merry way. NO! What God wants us to do is to partner with Him. Learn from our experiences so we will grow stronger each time a new challenge comes our way. He wants us to see where we came from and how we have grown. He wants us to trust Him in every situation and learn to lean on Him and walk in the boldness that He will give us if we indeed trust in Him for it. He wants us to wake up in the morning and choose to be different; choose to walk in the manner He created us to. By waving a magic wand we learn nothing. But walking the journey with Him we learn much!

How you choose to respond to your insecurities will make all the difference. Be strong and courageous! Be strong and courageous! Be strong and courageous! Choose to be who He created you to be!

DAY 28 | Challenge

Today's Date: _____

1.   Write out your declaration on how you are going to live your life from here on out!

_____

_____

_____

_____

_____

_____

_____

_____

Things I Learned About Myself Today.

Today's Date: _____

_____

_____

_____

_____

_____

_____

_____

_____

_____

_____

_____

_____

_____

_____

_____

_____

_____

_____

_____

DAY 29

Becoming A Giant Slayer Pt 1

Becoming A Giant Slayer Pt 1

Truth To Stand On:

For we are God's handiwork, created in Christ Jesus to do good works, which God prepared in advance for us to do.
–Ephesians 2:10 (NIV)

So here we are, can you believe it? So close to the end of this journey together! These last 2 days I have done in parts 1 & 2. The bible story I am using to finish off our journey is powerful and has so much in it that I believe we can use it as an anchor to solidify and hold us in our new-found assurance of who we are in Christ!

In the book of 1 Samuel is the famous story of David and Goliath. David was a young man who was still living at home, taking care of the sheep while the older brothers were off fighting the enemy. In this day and age being a sheepherder was considered to be one of the lowest paying jobs to have, much like that of a farmer. David's brothers looked down on their brother and really didn't have much use for him. David's dad sent his young son out to the battle ground to bring food for the brothers and check in to see how these mighty warriors were doing as they were to be fighting the Philistines. Of course, the brothers were rather irritated as older brothers get by their younger brothers "spying" on them. David's intention truly was to simply bring food, find out how the brothers were coping, and head back to let their dad know all was well. But God had another plan!

As the story goes we find out that David overheard the giant, Goliath challenging the Israelites to a battle but none of them would accept the challenge due to fear. They all sat on the sidelines listening to this monster of a man terrorize them and completely denounce the power of God. David became furious and decided that it was his obligation to destroy this giant!

David was looked upon by the army, and Saul, the king, in the same manner as many of us who struggle with insecurities feel; insignificant, inadequate and unable. But David was determined in his mind to fight for the honour of his God!

Now here is where the story gets very interesting. Since everyone thought David was incapable they decided to give him their best advice on he should fight this battle. Wearing Saul's armour seemed like a good idea to all. Of course, the armour was not made for David's small body structure, but for Saul's so it did not fit correctly and hung on him like a potato sack. I want to just pause here in the story for a moment. How many times have we wanted to accomplish a task and had someone else try to tell us how to do it because they thought we weren't capable in our own abilities? Or, how many of us have taken on someone else's ways and ideas because we thought ourselves incapable and ill equipped?

I can remember when I first started my speaking journey. I would watch other women preachers and try so hard to mimic many of them. If they were funny I would try to up my game in the funny department; if they were serious and direct I would then flip and try to be more direct and harsh. It was a rollercoaster ride of me trying to fit into someone else's armour! I often would begin the message I was about to preach with the statement something along the lines of, "Oh, by the way, just a warning; I am weird!" Feeling like for some reason I had to prepare everyone for what was about to come and if they thought I was weird or strange in any way, well I guess they were warned! HAHA! After many moments like these I had a very dear friend who has been in my life for many years come up to me and put me in my place. She said to me "Wendy, you have a gift of preaching and you need to stop making excuses for your personality!" BAMMMMM! Yes, message received, thank you very much! HAHAHA! Sometimes we need to hear these words from someone we trust and respect. From that moment on I stopped making excuses for who I was and how I preached. And I began to stop trying to be like someone else and finally allowed the Lord to direct me in how He created me to be and preach as he had intended me to preach! And now that I do that, my messages are more powerful and authentic because it is me being me, and not me wearing someone else's armour!

My friend and I often chuckle at this story because she doesn't remember saying this to me, nor can she believe she actually had the nerve! But I take it as a God moment! God spoke through her that day very clearly. And it was a day that changed my life.

So, I pass on the same message to you today! Don't live life trying to fit in to someone else's armour! Be who Christ created you to be. God created you to be YOU! And that is AWESOME!

DAY 29 | Challenge

Today's Date: _____

1. Have you ever found yourself trying to be like someone else to fit in?
   Or have you had someone else try to change who you are to fit in?
   (wearing someone else's armour) If yes, write down your experience
   here.
2. Now write out a bold statement to yourself like the one my friend said
   to me!

_____

_____

_____

_____

_____

_____

Things I Learned About Myself Today.

Today's Date: _____

_____

_____

_____

_____

_____

_____

_____

_____

_____

_____

_____

_____

_____

_____

_____

_____

_____

_____

DAY 30

Becoming A Giant Slayer Pt 2

Becoming A Giant Slayer Pt 2

Truth To Stand On:

Behold, I have given you authority to tread on serpents and scorpions, and over all the power of the enemy, and nothing shall hurt you.
–Luke 10:19 (NIV)

Today is a day of celebration! Today we slay our giant once and for all! Today we not only slay our giant, but we decapitate it, so it is dead and has no more life or hold on us! Are you READY?!

As we continue on in our story of David and Goliath we see that David approaches the giant with boldness and authority. He knew the power he had with God on his side, and he knew his Lord would not let him down. David was ready to put an end to this giant of a man who was terrorizing his nation. He knew the insults and the fear Goliath had brought to the Israelites had to come to a final end, and today was the day!

David took what he knew and what he felt comfortable with to fight this battle. He took a simple slingshot and some stones. I am sure there would have been a groan of defeat among the Israelite army before the challenge even began, when they saw what David was going to use as his weapon. Goliath himself laughed at David's choice of defense. Sound familiar? The enemy will laugh at us when we tell him, "This is it, you are going down!" He will laugh at us and try to put thoughts into our minds that we are too weak and come ill equipped to fight this giant. But just as David approached with boldness and authority, so shall we do the same!

David told Goliath that he is no longer going to speak against God or God's chosen people any longer. And with that statement he whirled his sling and stone and struck Goliath down. Now here is where the story gets even more interesting again; the best part! David approaches his enemy. He doesn't know with 100% assurance that his enemy is dead or simply knocked unconscious. But he takes that step of faith (a few very scary steps) forward towards his fallen foe. Pause here for a moment and think about what may have been going on in David's mind. David was possibly thinking and wondering if Goliath will get back up again as he approaches. What is going to happen in the time it takes him to get close enough to this giant to make sure he is in fact dead.

The key point to notice here is that David doesn't just knock down his giant and run; he approaches the giant to make sure he is dead. When he gets to his giant he pulls out the giant's own sword and uses that very sword to decapitate him! He made sure, 100% sure, that this giant was dead and would never, I repeat, never terrorize the Israelites ever again!

And so, my dear friends, my question to you on this last day of our journey together is: Are you ready to decapitate your giant and make sure it is dead, and will never terrorize you again?!

How many of us have prayed and prayed and went to the altar and prayed again for the Lord to take away these feelings of inadequacy and insecurities? Only to have them return again, alive and well. We need to decapitate our giants once and for all! God is here with you just as he was with David. But it was David who chose to take the step of faith and approach the giant with the confidence in knowing that God went with him. He didn't just sit back and say, "OK God, can you take this giant away?" No, he stepped forward in confidence, as a team with God and drew strength from God to bring final defeat over this giant!

Today is the day you choose to join the team with God and take that step forward towards your giant and finally decapitate him, so he no longer has power over you! No more simply knocking him down, today we make sure he is dead! Today is the day you claim victory over all your insecurities and rise up to be the Giant Slayer God has created you to be!

Prayer For Today:

Lord, today I become a giant slayer. I thank you for giving me the power and strength I need to defeat this enemy! Today I take that step of faith with you at my side and I put to death all the insecurities I have struggled with. I know I cannot do this on my own. So, I join forces with you along this journey and ask that you give me what I need each and every day to remain strong in you. I choose today to believe that I am perfectly and wonderfully made by you, my perfect creator. I choose to remember that you don't make junk! Amen!

DAY 30 | Challenge

Today's Date: _____

1. Write out a declaration to yourself and to the Lord that today is the day you choose to be a giant slayer.
2. Find a small flat stone and write on it in marker the words "I am a Giant Slayer". Keep this rock in a place you will see it often to remind

_____

_____

_____

_____

_____

_____

_____

_____

Things I Learned About Myself Along This 30 Day Journey.

Today's Date: _____

_____

_____

_____

_____

_____

_____

_____

_____

_____

_____

_____

_____

_____

_____

_____

_____

_____

_____

Until Next Time

Conclusion

Well Friends we have come to the end of our journey together. But this is not the end of your journey!!! Can I encourage you to keep on believing all the truths you have learned these past 30 days!!! You truly are beautifully and wonderfully made!!!

Choose to live each day in VICTORY!! You ARE a Giant Slayer!!!

In chapter 21, you were challenged in your relationship with Jesus. If you have never made a commitment to follow Him or if you have walked away from that commitment can I encourage you to take that step of faith and allow Christ back in your life! (Please read prayer at the bottom). He so wants to have a relationship with you! Open your heart up to Him and seek Him out!! He will show Himself real to you!! Find a bible believing church you can plug into. Contact me through my web page if you need any encouragement or guidance at all! I'm here to help!!!

If you prayed this prayer for the first time or as a re-commitment, please be sure to let me know!!!

Blessings to you all!!!
I pray this book blessed you as much as it did me to write it!!!

Wendy

Salvation Prayer

Dear Lord,
I want to know you more. I ask that you come into my life and show me that you are real. I thank you that you went to the cross so that I can have forgiveness of sin! And I ask that you come into my heart today! Lead and guide me through this life's journey! Thank you that you love me unconditionally!!! I look forward to all that you have for me from this day forward!!
Amen

My Weight Loss Journey Update

Made it to a total of 35 lbs down. Working on the last 20.
Stay tuned for the next book. The journey will be
complete by then I'm sure!!! HAHA!!!

Meet Wendy Payne

 Wendy has an engaging personality that cannot soon be forgotten. Her zeal, vibrancy and love for life can be seen in her ministry, work and family. Her desire for others to experience the power of God in their own life is contagious to those who have the opportunity to hear her speak. She loves to preach the word in such a way that people really understand and grasp the heart of the message.

With over 30 years of ministry experience and credentialed with the Pentecostal Assemblies of Canada, Wendy has had the opportunity to minister to people in all walks of life. A well-experienced motivator that speaks at retreats, conferences, camp meetings and workshops.

In 2015, Wendy, her husband Darrel; along with their daughter Tamara had the opportunity to plant a church on Manitoulin Island in northern Ontario. Wendy serves as the Lead Pastor to this young, growing church body. She is very well known in the community, not only for the great ministry she does as 'Pastor Wendy', but also for her work as a licensed hairstylist, allowing her ministry to reach further and deeper.

Wendy has been married for over 30 years to Darrel, who you will always find supporting her and working behind the scenes. She is also a mother of three daughters and 'Oma' (grandma) to three grand babies who she adores!

Wendy loves to laugh and enjoys her walk with God every day. She has a passion for people to know God and strengthen their relationships with Him. She is a must-see and if you have the opportunity to say "Hi", do it. She will make the moment worth it.

Contact Wendy

Pastor / Author / Motivational Speaker

wendy.contagiouspower@gmail.com
www.contagiouspower.ca

#pastor_wendy | @ContagiousPowerCanada

Watch for the next book release!

Entitled

"Contagious Power"

Wendy will take you on a journey through biblical
stories that show of God's Contagious Power in
situations that looked IMPOSSIBLE. She will teach you
that Gods Power is as alive today as it was then.

A Daylon C. Clark

PUBLISHING COMPANY

WWW.DAYLONCLARK.COM

Use the inner giftings [spiritual talents and abilities]
that God has given you to
serve [minister to and to bless] others.

– 1 Peter 4:10

CPSIA information can be obtained
at www.ICGtesting.com
Printed in the USA
FFOW04n1634020418
46137686-47226FF

9 780994 064349